A LITTLE LEARNING

A LITTLE LEARNING

by Walter J. Handren, S.J.

Saint Joseph's College
Philadelphia, Pennsylvania

THE NEWMAN PRESS
WESTMINSTER, MARYLAND
1956

Imprimi potest: WILLIAM F. MALONEY, S.J.
Provincial
Maryland Province of the Society of Jesus

Nihil obstat: JOSEPH A. M. QUIGLEY
Censor Librorum
September 28, 1955

Imprimatur: ✠ JOHN F. O'HARA, C.S.C., D.D.
Archbishop of Philadelphia
October 1, 1955

TO
SAINT IGNATIUS
OF
LOYOLA

Preface

M ANY students set out on their college careers with all the good will in the world. Gifted with the desire to learn, they try their best, but they do not quite know what to do or how to do it. Some, baffled by the seeming complexity of the educational process, subside at once and drift through their courses, compensating by deriving as much fun as they can from "college life." Others, made of sterner stuff, keep plugging away heroically throughout their four years, gradually acquiring a rough and ready method of educating themselves, but at the cost of entirely too much effort and with a great waste of time. It is with the intention of helping all these men of good will that the author presents this book.

It has been envisioned as a small handbook which the student can keep close by for ready reference throughout his four years of college. Each of its three divisions has a distinct work to perform. The first part gives a survey of the entire scholastic background against which the student will work out his destiny during the ensuing months. The purpose, at this point, is to describe for the student all the important details of the average Catholic college environment in order that, being forewarned, he may be better equipped to adjust himself rapidly and efficiently to his surroundings.

The second part moves on to a discussion of the six essential areas of human life which must be the objectives of all satisfactory educational training. Admittedly, the expansion of this section might well have been carried on until it reached the status of a complete volume. Yet, we think the student has been offered enough information to permit him to apply the instructions to his curriculum in a manner calculated to obtain the best results from the study of each subject. This section is, therefore, a philosophy of education designed for the student.

Part three aims to apply to the concrete particulars of the student's everyday study activities the general principles inculcated in the two preceding sections. We have tried to select rules for study which will solve all the basic difficulties. We admit that many more concrete and particular rules could have been given, but that would have meant lengthening this part of the book beyond all measure, thus, perhaps sacrificing clarity to superfluity of detail. We have limited ourselves to essentials. Their understanding and their employment will, we believe, result in clearing up most of the incidental troubles which beset the average student. One who attempts to apply thoroughly *all* the suggestions given here will hardly be left with any real difficulties, unless he is an abnormal case. For the rest, each student must learn his own tricks-of-the-trade; these will be of more help to him than those taught him by another.

The best results should be derived from using this manual as a textbook in an orientation course for freshmen. Groups of from fifteen to twenty could meet once a week for fifty minutes through both semesters of the school year, under the direction of faculty advisors. During these meetings, the advisors should explain the book, create discussion on the problems which arise, and assign projects for practice. There need be no examinations because the course would be purely extracurricular.

In addition to attending the group meetings, each freshman would be expected to confer from time to time with the advisor under whom he is studying. At these consultations, personal problems having a bearing on college life in all its phases would be the subject matter. At the end of the year the advisors would be asked to submit to the Dean progress reports on each of the freshmen. This same system might also be used with profit on those high school seniors who plan to enter college.

But the usefulness of *A Little Learning* need not be restricted to those persons who are taking guided courses in its subject matter. It may still be studied effectively by mature students who lack supervision, provided they are sufficiently interested in furthering their education. For instance, those attending evening college, or taking courses in adult education, or even those who are no longer in school, but who are privately following some course of study out of personal interest or to help themselves in their careers, may peruse the book with very beneficial results. What is needed for the successful study of this handbook is a serious desire to learn, coupled with the patience to work one's way slowly through its highly condensed contents.

It would be unfair to close these prefatory remarks without giving proper credit to Dr. Jane Furlong and Miss Grace McNelis for their part in the composition of this book. Not only did they relieve the author of the need to bother with many of the irritating details, but their sound learning and good judgment also proved invaluable in helping to arrange both the content and form to the greatest possible advantage.

WALTER J. HANDREN, S.J.

Saint Joseph's College
Nativity of Our Lady
September 8, 1955

Contents

✠⟫⟫-⟫⟫-⟫⟫⟪⟪-⟪⟪-⟪⟪

Preface   vii

Prologue: Ave Frater . . . !   1

PART I. THE ENVIRONMENT

   I.   *What Is College Anyway?*   11

  II.   *Growing Out of High School*   17

 III.   *To Cram or Not to Cram*   21

 IV.   *Rubbing Elbows with the Experts*   27

  V.   *Growing Also in Grace*   31

 VI.   *Extra! Extra! Extracurriculars!*   37

 VII.   *Rah! Rah! Rah!*   43

VIII.   *The Old Alma Mater*   47

 IX.   *Browsing Around*   52

  X.   *Where Dwellest Thou?*   60

 XI.   *What Next?*   64

PART II. THE PHILOSOPHY

XII.	*A Human Approach*	73
XIII.	*Receiving Impressions*	80
XIV.	*Expressing Oneself*	94
XV.	*The Thought World*	105
XVI.	*The Necessity of Religion*	115
XVII.	*Aesthetic Development*	121
XVIII.	*The Significance of Discipline*	130

PART III. THE TECHNIQUE

XIX.	*Definite Goals*	141
XX.	*General Methods*	145
XXI.	*Reading*	155
XXII.	*Use of the Library*	161
XXIII.	*Powers of Observation*	169
XXIV.	*The Reason*	172
XXV.	*Inspiration*	177
XXVI.	*Attention*	180
XXVII.	*Memory*	187
XXVIII.	*Making Notes*	195
Epilogue: . . . Atque Vale!		205
Index		209

PROLOGUE

Ave Frater . . . !

I T IS good to know that you are going to attend a
Catholic college and complete your education
in the proper manner. Today there is more need
than ever for well educated Catholic laymen—men
who will be a credit to themselves and to the
Church in secular matters, and who will also have
such a thorough grasp of their religion that they
will be able to give glory to God in the everyday
conduct of their lives. Your choosing a Catholic
college indicates that you wish to be numbered
among men of this type.

In spite of everything, a college education is
still a precious thing. Even though our American
system of mass-production has vulgarized it, making it all too common, it continues to be a vitally
important stage in the life of the average young
man. More and more high school students are looking forward to a college education as the normal
and necessary completion of their schooling; yet,
as in the case of many other things taken for
granted, its point can be missed unless serious
efforts be made to grasp it.

The approach to college, therefore, should be

deliberate and thoughtful. There should be no blithe acceptance of it as one's due, no blind plunging ahead into its social or athletic whirl, no view of class and recitations as a disagreeable but inevitable price to pay for the more pleasant side of the life. You who are desirous of a college degree might weigh well the famous words of Alexander Pope in his *Essay on Criticism:*

A little learning is a dangerous thing;
Drink deep, or taste not the Pierian spring:
There shallow draughts intoxicate the brain,
And drinking largely sobers us again.

The point is obvious. There is no one more futile than a half-educated man. He has deluded himself into the belief that he has something which, in reality, he does not have at all. In college he sauntered along, sipping casually from the fount of learning. Graduated, at length, he sallied forth to do battle with life's problems under the false assumption that he was fully educated. His number is legion, and lives of confusion, frustration, and failure attest to the infrequency of true education among such.

The difficulty, we would say, arises out of a wrong approach to college. Present-day students seem to be looking for the wrong thing, probably because no one has ever taken the pains to explain to them what education really is or what they are supposed to respond to. Oftentimes, when they are questioned, the reasons they give for attending college betray their misunderstanding of its purpose. Either they profess to be trying to learn how to make money, and they want a degree which is said to be the open door to profitable positions; or, with tongue in cheek, they give some memorized formula, supposed to define education, and then proceed to pay attention only to those subjects directly connected with money-making, ending up the whole farce without a semblance of an education.

There are other mental attitudes manifested in taking up college life. Some students enroll at a certain college merely because their parents, who hold the purse strings, insist on it. The result of this is a spiritless attendance at a place in which they have no interest. Some few come to college in the hope of a temporary postponement of military service. In this instance, the intention is to run away from something. Both of these attitudes are negative and, as such, will prevent the attainment of a true education.

Whatever your view of education or your motives for going to college, approach the contents of this book with an open mind. It has been written in an endeavor to give the Catholic college student a proper understanding of the meaning of education. The author, having been in contact with undergraduates many years, has been staggered by the tremendous waste of money, time, talent, energy, even lives, which is accepted as commonplace in the realm of the schools. It is no wonder that there is heard the rumble of the distant drum.

Education in the United States is at present under heavy fire; this is due, we believe, to the fact that those who have the supervision of it are not paying attention to its real meaning. Although the concern of education is the making of a *complete man*—just that and nothing more—yet, in our country, it seems to be used as a means to everything but that. The position of Catholicism is especially good in that we Catholics have an illustrious tradition in the field of education stretching back over a thousand years. Our methods are still valid because they are based on eternally true principles and aimed, now as always, at completing the man. We never attempt merely to train some sort of operative for a job which may not even be in existence tomorrow. But (and this is a very big *but*), for our education to have its full effect, the student must be willing to cooperate with it. He must be willing to inconvenience himself, to suffer some pangs: for "knowledge maketh a bloody entrance."

It will be very easy for you, during your course, to fall into the "wait and cram" system, to delight in getting away with as much as you can—as though education were a sort of contest between student and professor. You may become entranced by the spirit of fun and adventure which makes you search constantly for a good time, thus failing to strive for the attainment of the best possible standing. The line of least resistance will always be there for you to follow, and there will never be wanting plenty of students to urge you to wander along its pleasant paths. The usual sediment of irresponsibles will hold that you are young only once and you may as well enjoy yourself while you may. "Hard work and money-grubbing are for later," they will say; "why waste your youth anticipating the monotony of old age?"

Another insidious enemy which will prevent the attainment of a good education is the almost universal attitude of depression and frustration found today among the young. They seem to be crushed by the feeling that life is useless and not worth the struggle. The reason given is that they will either have to go into military service and "waste" several years, or, if they escape that (or, if and when they have finished it!), they face an almost insurmountable economic barrier to marriage and the rearing of a family.

That the difficulties are enormous no one would deny. But, you should have the spirit of combat. You should not permit yourself to be stopped by man-made evils before you begin. What man has done he can undo! The path may be long and full of suffering, but only the coward runs from suffering when great deeds are to be done, and an eternal prize to be won. You, who profess to follow Christ, should not sit back hopelessly while evil men take over and dominate God's world. You should be willing to pay any price for the triumph of good over evil.

It is to prevent you from starting college life in this wasteful fashion that these lines are being written. Too often have we seen juniors and seniors fail because they acted unwisely during their freshman and sophomore years. The course becomes more difficult as you go on if you do not prepare from the beginning by hard and constant study. Any initial carelessness on your part will catch up with you later. The words of the poet Omar are peculiarly apt when applied in this context:

> The moving finger writes and, having writ,
> Moves on: nor all your piety nor wit
> Shall lure it back to cancel half a line,
> Nor all your tears wash out a word of it.

The following pages will go into the matter in detail. With these few words of counsel, we desire to incite more students to attend college with the proper motives, and to take the correct means, *from the start*, of attaining the goals of a college education. If we accomplish this for some well-intentioned but uninstructed beginners, the effort will not have been in vain. We hope you will profit by your four years in college, that you will take your vocation as a student seriously, and that you will apply yourself to becoming the best man you possibly can—with the grace of God and the help the faculty can give you.

PART I

The Environment

⇛⇛⇛⟫⟩⟨⟨⟪⟪⟪

CHAPTER I

What Is College Anyway?

➤➤➤➤➤➤➤➤◀◀◀◀◀◀

RIDICULOUS as it seems, it is possible to complete a college course, obtain a degree, and still not know the meaning of a college education. To forestall such a dire fate we pause before considering your scholastic future, item by item, in order to treat the more general topic: what is college all about?

You know that education extends through elementary school, high school, and college, and you may sometimes ask yourself why it is necessary to attend successively three different kinds of school. The question becomes even more pertinent when you notice that the same subjects are frequently taught in all three. For instance, English, history, religion, and some form of the study of our government are subjects studied from the beginning to the end of the educational journey. Why is that?

The reason for dividing the educational process into three stages follows upon the needs of man's nature. The grade school is adapted to the *child*; the high school presents its subjects according to the needs of the *adolescent*; the purpose of the college is to educate the *young adult*. As you grow, your problems change and your needs differ according to your age. Since your physical self gradually develops and affects your whole person, you learn differently as life progresses. In addition to this, there are some subjects which you are not prepared to learn until you have reached a certain maturity.

Let us take religion as a case in point. In grade school the study of this subject comprises only the fundamentals, with memory work the main task, since only superficial intellectual comprehension is to be expected. Moral problems are infrequent among children and we teach them the simple doctrine suited to them. Adolescence arrives during high school, with a consequent increase in moral problems. Now is the time for the careful presentation of moral theology, and dogma must be given with reasoned argument—but still not abstrusely. Finally, at the college level, young people are presumed to have reached the peak of their intellectual possibilities. They may be given all the religion they have time to study, and it may be presented from every possible viewpoint. What we have said here of religion during the three stages of schooling applies in like manner to any other subject treated successively in the three schools.

The function of any school is to help impart an education. We say *help*, because the school cannot do it entirely alone. Education is a social process, and all things in life contribute to it—parents, school, Church, the State, the person himself, life in general. These assist in the complete formation of the person, and this we call education. Although many of its ingredients come from without, a true education begins and develops within a man. It is a mysterious growth which takes place within the mind and body after a man has received a number of varied and significant sense impressions. He turns these data over and over in his mind, combines, orders, and makes them part of himself, so that, after a while, he finds himself instinctively acting according to what he has "learned."

Therefore, we may say that an education makes you different. Because of it, you become something other than what you were before. Being something different, you will act differently, whether or not you realize it. Training, on the other hand, teaches you how to *do* something. It does not attempt to make you over, but merely points toward a situation and prepares you for it. We may sum up by saying that training is for occasional benefit, education is for life.

We also hear the distinction made between formal and informal education. Informal education looks to the everyday aspect of things. It is accomplished without any particular order or method; it is not conducted in school. It happens incidentally, as a secondary effect of some other process, and its success depends largely upon the individual's alertness. We may well define it as the dialectic of the human person with his environment.

Formal education, on the other hand, concerns itself with the more profound aspects of certain essential attitudes and operations of human beings, and bodies of human knowledge. It is called *formal* because it is primarily and directly concerned with the total development of the whole man, and because, over the years, certain set means, methods, times, and places have been found best for its accomplishment. It needs experts to hand on formal education because not everyone has the ability to do so, nor have they taken the time to learn how to transmit that which they themselves have learned. Only a few have the talent for passing on to others, clearly and forcefully, the subject-matter of what we call a formal education.

A college has as its purpose to present the basic subjects of formal education in a way fitted to the mentality of young adults. The college may also offer other subjects in addition to the essential ones, but these will usually be by way of further training not necessary to education. Or, at least, they will not be of first consideration in the educational process. The purpose of the college is not primarily to offer that which will directly help to make a living. Its primary purpose is to teach you to live. Normally speaking, a healthy man will do a better job than a sickly one, and so, too, an educated man will conduct himself more efficiently than one who is merely trained. Subjects which are for training only should be added to education, not substituted for it. To be more concrete, an educated man will make a better doctor, lawyer, business man, than a man who has been merely trained, no matter how thoroughly, in those professions.

Training should be left to the trade, professional, and graduate schools. By the time a student has reached the graduate level, he may be considered to have received all his basic formal education. The graduate school may then feel free to concentrate its efforts toward specialization in a more restricted area. Thus shall we continue to have experts in all fields.

Your reaction to college should be in accordance with the aims of the college, not against them. If your purposes are contrary to those of the school, honesty will demand that you do not matriculate. You should not enter college, then, with a consuming desire to learn how to make more and more money, or to be taught how to get a job and hold it. These things will probably be treated along the way because of the additional training subjects found in most colleges, but they may not stand out as being considered very important. If you have thought enough of the college to entrust your education to it, you should be consistent and trust the college's method of achieving it. A wise man will, accordingly, cooperate fully with all the rules of his school because he understands that everything will have its purpose toward his education.

Many strange reasons are given as the deciding factors in the choice of a particular college. Some students are fascinated by successful athletic teams; others feel more kindly disposed toward a college which is conveniently located; while still others know a successful business man who once attended the school of their choice. These viewpoints are, to say the least, short-sighted. They emphasize things which have nothing to do with the educational qualities of a school. For, when you, as an alumnus, are faced with the necessity of charting your own course through life and weathering its storms, it will be of no practical benefit to you that your college always won its football games, or that it was located one bus fare from home, or that it numbers many business tycoons among its alumni. These things are but the trimmings of education —pretty, but unnecessary. The important thing will be: what did the college give you which will carry you through this present crisis?

A reasonable way of selecting your college is to inspect the curriculum and question the aims of the college in order to see if they coincide with your purpose in attending. Ask people whose judgment you trust what opinion they have of this school. Do they think it accomplishes its aims? Having gathered the evidence, form your own judgment. The reasons for your choice will color your whole approach to college life.

CHAPTER II

Growing Out of
High School

≫≫-≫≫-≫≫«-«-«-«

Now that you have finished your high school
course, you are entering upon that longest,
busiest, and most difficult stage of human life—
adulthood. From now on you will be expected to
face the world with self-reliance. Responsibilities
will come and remain with you. Problems will develop. Worries will blossom. But you must not run
away from life. On the contrary, you must face it
squarely, grow with it, master it. To educate you
to this frame of mind is the work of the college.

One of the first things you must do is to cut the
strings which bind you to the high school. You
cannot acquire the "college way" unless you throw
yourself wholeheartedly into its life. Things are
done differently here, and you must catch on
quickly if you do not wish to be left behind. You
cannot proceed with one foot in high school and
the other in college. That attitude will block all
progress. It may cost you a few pangs to admit it,
but you are no longer a student in your beloved
high school. You are an alumnus, and that means
you now have other worlds to conquer.

Increasing maturity is the mark of the college man. This will appear in various guises according to the need of the moment. For example, in college life, there is less supervision of activities, either in or out of the classroom. The extra-curricular activities are run by the students themselves. If the students fail in their responsibilities, the activity fails, because the moderator will not do their work for them. Of course, there is some supervision because it is an educational process, but there is much less than in high school. The supervision given has as its purpose to stimulate and guide, not to do the work.

A growing power of self-analysis should begin to manifest itself during your college years. You should become increasingly able to detect your weaknesses, to reflect on the reasons for them, and to suggest to yourself practicable remedies for their cure. Admittedly, not everyone will have the same ability to do this. Some are gifted with greater powers of introspection than others. But each one of us has some of it, and we are responsible before God for developing that which He has given us.

A practical result of growth in self-analysis will be the lessening of the "gang spirit." In high school, students are wont to gang together much as they did when they were small boys. This comes from the feeling of uncertainty all children have at facing the world. The college proposes to draw out all the qualities of self-reliance a young man may have. You, on your part, will show that you are profiting by the education you are receiving if you become too individualistic to travel in gangs. Note well the difference between the spirit of cooperation and the gang spirit. We may illustrate it as follows: you have the spirit of cooperation when you will do with and for others whatever you would do openly and by yourself. You have the spirit of the gang when you would be afraid to do a certain thing openly or by yourself, but will not hesitate when supported by the gang.

Another realm in which you will discover marked differences between the college and the high school is in the classroom and study technique. Most college instructors will use the lecture system, and you may be in class for quite some time without the instructor mentioning your name, except in calling the roll. You will sit there, period after period, alert to everything that happens, taking careful notes on the lecture, just one of the group. No one will exhort you to study, nor will anyone check to see if you are studying. Every so often a written test will be given and the marks duly recorded. But at mid-term the day of reckoning will come when the grades are passed out. It is so easy to be lulled into a false sense of security during the semester that it takes a student who is maturing properly to avoid it.

You are expected, therefore, to take care of yourself. You are supposed to enter into the spirit of the life, and not to have to be coaxed along like a stubborn child. In the beginning, the college way may strike you as a cold, indifferent sort of system, wherein no one cares whether or not you survive.

This feeling will pass. It is due mainly to the contrast between your late lofty status as a high school senior, and your present position as the lowest of the low—a college freshman. If you forget about your feelings and apply yourself steadily you will soon notice that people are paying attention to you, that you are not forgotten, alone, lost. You are merely being asked to stand upon your own two feet, be a man, and "join the fellows."

CHAPTER III

To Cram or Not to Cram

❯❯❯-❯❯❯-❯❯❯❮❮❮-❮❮❮-❮❮❮

How mysterious it is that people invest the years and labor they do in a college education and then persistently use all the means available to prevent themselves from getting it! For, a college education is an investment. You and your parents have set aside four important years—years in which you might be doing something very worthwhile—in order to blueprint your future. You, my friend, are the only one who can make this investment pay off. Neither your parents nor your teachers, nor even God Himself, can do anything about it if you choose to waste your college years. You have it in your power to turn time into something beyond all evaluation—an educated man.

The deciding factor in the whole business is study, constant, hard, persistent study. You may use what fulsome terms you like in describing your appreciation of college, but your speech will jangle emptily unless you give it reality by the substance of your study. You may get your grades without too much work, and you may thus come by your diploma; that is due to the peculiar system of judging spiritual values by mathematical symbols in vogue in this country. But no one, no, not even you yourself, will consider you an educated man unless you have faced your subjects and mastered them. You may profit, therefore, if we discuss some attitudes toward study in college.

Learning is not easy. There is no known way (if those who write "How to . . ." books are honest) of making it simple and pleasant. The good student often experiences a kind of savage satisfaction from slugging his way through an especially thick section of the matter, but that doesn't make subsequent study a thing of delight. Patience and method help to lighten the burden, but they do not remove it. You, who have chosen college as a career, must expect to work. If you try to attain your goal any other way, you will cheat yourself.

The most prevalent and most successful temptation against study is cramming, the evil genius of the campus. No one could accurately estimate the harm done by this refuge of the lazy. Its power to hurt comes from the false sense of accomplishment it leaves you with. You can pass examinations by means of cramming, but that is about the only good it can be credited with. Being a system of rapid memorization rather than study, it never helps you to learn a subject. Learning is a growth and, as such, must be slow.

Cramming is, educationally speaking, a waste. It leaves empty spaces in your mind, just as stuffing clothes into a suitcase fails to utilize all the available space. Remove the clothes, fold and replace them in orderly fashion, and you will find more space still left. Orderly, methodical study gives you the opportunity to see many more connections and associations and, thus, to hold more matter coherently in your mind.

Did it ever occur to you to think of cramming as an attempt at the impossible? The teacher, an expert, takes a whole semester to do what you expect to accomplish in a few hours! He has explained, expounded, clarified, drilled, questioned, and restated the matter for weeks; you have gone over it intensively for a day or so. Do you expect to master your subject by that method? And, if you say that your cramming is merely a refreshing of your mind on matter already studied or learned, the natural question follows: "How studied or learned? By previous cramming?"

In contrast to cramming, the study of a subject from day to day facilitates the mastery of it. Careful, progressive study makes memorization easy and develops the habit of review, which is an essential of learning. You must be convinced personally of the value of regular study habits if you are to adopt them, because in college no one supervises your study to the degree that it was done in high school. Now you are supposed to have the initiative to form your own plans and accomplish your own objectives. If you start studying with method and perseverance the first week of freshman classes, you will be giving yourself a wonderful training for life. Life itself must be faced with method and perseverance if you are to succeed at it, for life moves steadily on and does not wait for anyone. If you are not alive to the passing opportunities, you will be left behind.

You will find that some of your classmates will scoff at you for studying constantly. They will try to break down your resistance and make you as lazy as they are. But, remember that anyone who stands out from the rank and file in this world will be laughed at from time to time. If you intend to accomplish anything worthwhile, you must be prepared to ignore the ridicule and follow the path you know to be the right one. This takes moral courage, but it is part of the price you must pay for success.

Important as a means of building up your eagerness for study is the habit of noting the relationships which exist between the various subjects in the curriculum. You should make positive efforts to see where, for example, religion and government react upon each other; what bearing the study of foreign languages has upon the understanding of history; where the different treatises of scholastic philosophy are needed in order to clarify the view in sociological problems; how the ethics course should be applied to the multiple fields of business practice. If you make this effort to integrate the curriculum for yourself, you will have gone far toward giving yourself strong incentives to get the maximum out of your studies. This system will supply you with targets to shoot at which will be especially valuable because you will have set them up for yourself.

In actual life no one subject stands in complete

isolation from all others; if in the field of education they are so separated, this has been artificially induced, and the artificiality will work to the detriment of education. Sometimes you can get help in working out this integration from an instructor. Some teachers are particularly good at giving hints of this kind even during their class-periods. You should keep alert to pick up all you can on this subject.

An important part of the art of study includes the ability to get the most out of class. Here, promptness is a big step in the right direction. Not only do late-comers disturb the class and the teacher (if they are permitted to enter the room), but they also destroy the continuity of the lecture for themselves. Class is one of the most important aids to learning, and you, the student, are expected to understand this. The instructor has prepared his matter and has something to say. Since he is an authority on the subject, the beginner should want to hear all he has to say about it.

Therefore, you should permit yourself to be late or absent only when you cannot avoid it. You should never have to rely on someone else's notes. You may object that the "cut system," which is in force at many colleges, seems to indicate that a certain number of absences will not make much difference. Reasoning of this sort shows a lack of understanding of the meaning of this system. The allowance of cuts means that until a student has missed a certain number of classes he is still eligible to take the examinations and is not to be made to repeat the course. But is not intended to encourage absence from class. The ideal student will not miss any class if he can help it.

As a final word: in this mechanized age, when technology is second nature, it is not asking too much to suggest that all students should be able to typewrite—at least by the "two-finger" system. This accomplishment will prove beneficial not only for keeping a businesslike set of notes, but will aid in the important practice of submitting attractive term papers. Typewriters are common nowadays, and elderly ones are easily acquired second-hand. Their worth may be measured by higher grades.

CHAPTER IV

Rubbing Elbows with the Experts

>>>->>>->>><<<-<<<-<<<

ONE way to make college life miserable for your-self is to consider your teachers your oppo-nents. Many students do this. They begin their college careers with the firm conviction that all professors have as their objective to see that their students fail, that all tests and examinations are traps to catch the unwary, and that death is pref-erable to permitting the teacher to put across any of his theories. This stand may lend a spirit of ad-venture to college life, but there is little else to recommend it. There is no need to condemn such an obvious fallacy, but perhaps there is some need to indicate the positive harm which may come of it.

You are a wise student if you realize you have before you four years in which to associate with ex-perts in many fields. College professors have to be good in order to get their jobs and keep them. They are men with a deep interest in certain spheres of learning, and they have gone to great pains to make themselves thoroughly at home in them. In addition to this, God has endowed them with the desire to help others to develop and become better. Not every human being has this desire or the ability to use it.

All professors, therefore, have much to give you. If you should foolishly take a childish attitude toward them, you would cut yourself off from many benefits not mentioned in the college catalog. A college teacher wields much of his influence (and, therefore, he teaches) out of class—in corridors, in the cafeteria, in informal discussion in his office. You had better not look on the teacher as your enemy if you wish to benefit by association with him.

When college days are over, you will never again have a like opportunity to consort with so many outstanding men interested in passing on to you all the knowledge and wisdom they can. In the business world your associates are too often your competitors. They are not eager, as a rule, to teach you anything for fear of your getting their jobs. But in college, to make you outstanding is the reason for the faculty's existence. You are the object of their fondest expectations. They spend most of their year thinking about you. Your success is theirs, and no one is more pleased than the teacher at his pupil's success.

Your classmates may sometimes regale you with lurid stories about professorial chicanery and the suffering of the students under administrative injustice. Enjoy the stories, by all means, but learn to edit them. Teachers *do* make mistakes, since they are human; and when mistakes are made, someone usually has to suffer. A mistake indicates frailty, not malice. A student who is unwilling to excuse and forget the occasional mistakes of his teachers can hardly call himself a man. He is still a child believing in fairy godmothers.

If you think you have it hard with your teachers, consider the task they have with you. It is proverbial that schoolboys are most unwilling learners, and, alas! college men seem to consider themselves perennial schoolboys. There are some subjects in which you will have a natural interest. There will be others in which you will not only have no interest, but toward which you will even have a well developed antipathy. Now, consider the plight of the teacher who is scheduled to teach you something you are mulishly convinced should not be in the curriculum. He is probably very fond of his subject and eager to interest and instruct others in it. He will wish to make the classroom a pleasant place while conducting the hard business of education, but you may be trying to turn it into a battleground on which, no matter what you seem to accomplish, you alone will suffer defeat.

Professors, in their enthusiasm for their subjects, may forgetfully pile too much work upon you, but it is always possible to talk over the difficulty with them. A declaration of war should be the last resort. You may also hear it said that a certain teacher is a "slave driver." Be sure to ask those who bring this grim report whether they have tried to keep up with him by pacing themselves in their *daily* study. They are only entitled to complain, you know, if they have tried and found by experience that they cannot keep up.

There are no statistics at hand, but it can be said, with all safety, that the number of students in the United States who have cracked under intensive study is very small. Those whose health has been broken have had something else wrong with them, in the majority of cases. Never be retarded by worry that your professor will drive you to an untimely grave by overwork. Having once been a student himself, he has some idea of what the student mind can bear.

Consultations with the professors should not be confined to the subject of studies. You should be ready to ask their help in many quarters. They are not only learned, but experienced. They can give you the benefit of their experience in many ways. The day of the "absent-minded professor" is ended, if, indeed, it ever existed. There may have been some professors who were wool-gatherers, but they would have been such no matter what career they chose to follow. The modern college instructor is wide awake and in contact with reality. He can give much sound advice and real help to those who wish to accept it.

CHAPTER V

Growing Also in Grace

⋙⋙⋙⋘⋘⋘

Pius XI once wrote in his encyclical on the
Christian Education of Youth: "Hence, the true
Christian, product of Christian education, is the
supernatural man who thinks, judges and acts constantly and consistently in accordance with right
reason illumined by the supernatural light of the
example and teaching of Christ." These words
sum up the objective of Catholic education and
give you the reason why spirituality and religion
play such an important part in it. The fully educated Catholic must be a supernatural man, one
who reflects Christ in his whole bearing. This cannot be attained by casual contact with religion, nor
will it be the result of formal courses in religion,
if the student simply takes them and does nothing
more. The danger in limiting religion to classroom courses is that it gives you the illusion that
you practice your religion. Because you have a theoretical appreciation of the Faith, you may falsely
assume that you are therefore a good Catholic,
whereas, in reality, you may rarely manifest any of
the effects of your knowledge.

Since knowledge, however, is a necessary prerequisite to performance, you will show that you are an unusually wise student if you study your religion courses as seriously as you do the others. One of the truly sad blunders committed by a great number of Catholic students is to consider religion the "snap" course, the "breather," something put into the curriculum because the college must make a gesture toward the Faith in order to maintain its name *Catholic*. Any college which has this attitude toward the formal study of the Catholic Faith (and we doubt that there are any) has an administration which is not in contact with reality. Such an institution is living in an unreal world. Its graduates will discover that eventually; in the meantime, it is misleading its students.

You will follow your convictions. If you are not first convinced of the Faith, you will not practice it. You may go through the empty motions of attendance at Mass and the reception of the sacraments, but the actions will have little or no meaning for you. The world today is dominated by ideas. Unfortunately, the really great men who have these ideas are too often bad men, and their ideas are bringing misery upon the nations. If the Catholic Faith is to make itself felt in the world, its "Idea," the Word of God, must be understood and be the dynamic force in your life and in the life of every Catholic. Only then will the Faith have its proper effect upon "those who sit in darkness and in the shadow of death. . ." (Luke 1:79).

Since we shall treat religion as a part of formal education at some length later in this book, we shall limit ourselves here to a discussion of the rest of the spiritual life of the students. You sometimes hear the question asked: "Why all the emphasis on spiritual extra-curricular activities? Isn't it bad enough to have to go to religion classes, without having to attend daily Mass, school retreats, sodality meetings, and the like?" We find ourselves with little sympathy for such questioners because their attitude indicates an almost total lack of understanding of their religion. If you were to read and study religious books assiduously until you knew the subject perfectly, and yet never went to Mass, Confession, Communion, or to any other formal exercise of your religion, you could hardly call yourself a Catholic. Knowledge is not enough. You are not a holy man by knowing how to be holy, nor are you a Catholic by knowing how to be one. Religion is not only knowing, but living; and life means activity. The idea goes further. Since religious life is real life, it is not intermittent; it must be continuous or it will die. For that reason you must practice your religion not only during formal religious exercises, but also throughout every single activity of your life.

Since most of these spiritual extra-curricular activities are optional, I would advise you, young man, to join one of them for the completion of your Catholic education. Do not miss the main point of your attending a Catholic college. The greatness of the institution does not consist in its courses in any of the secular subjects, no matter how well it conducts them, but in the Christian philosophy of life it teaches. The implanting of this philosophy extends beyond the limits of the classroom into the extra-curriculars, not the least of which are the religious activities.

The spiritual exercises included in the religious program are not merely pious trimmings added to the serious business of education. Man's purpose in life is to work for and with God at all times, and not only occasionally in an artificially created atmosphere. You, as a student, will be following a definite, though temporary, vocation. As religion must permeate all the activities of a man's life in the world, so also must it be found in all the activities of students, even in the extra-curriculars. God wants your cooperation and service *as a student,* not merely as a Sunday worshiper.

When you graduate, you will be expected to take your place in the parish as an educated and apostolic layman. You cannot prepare for that overnight, but you must grow into it. The college has the duty to train you for parish life by offering you activities similar to those you will find in a parish, so that you may develop through practice. Notice, you are expected to develop yourself; the school cannot *make* you anything: it can only assist you to *become* something.

With this intention in mind, the college will probably offer some of the following activities:

1. *Sodality of the Blessed Virgin.* This is a Catholic Action organization, originally founded exclusively for men, having as its purpose to honor

the Mother of God, to strive for the salvation and perfection of its members and their contemporaries, and to work for the defense of the Church. Its members are supposed to act as a leavening influence upon the environment in which they live.

2. *Confraternity of Christian Doctrine.* This apostolic group trains its members to teach religion to children. Since this will someday be your duty as a parent, you will receive an excellent preparation for your future career, in addition to doing untold good among the young while you are still in college.

3. *Holy Name Society.* In addition to reverence for the Name and Person of Jesus Christ, this group attempts to make Catholic men more "faith conscious" throughout their working day so that there is never a time when they are not aware of their Catholicity and the need of acting in accordance with it.

4. *Special devotions.* Under this heading we may include the Mass of the Holy Ghost which opens the school year; daily Mass for the convenience of those who can and wish to attend; occasional Benedictions; Way of the Cross during Lent; novenas at certain special times; and, finally, an annual three-day retreat which all the students are expected to attend.

This does not exhaust the list, but it is a good cross-section of the active spiritual life of the average Catholic college. If there are not more students participating in this program, the fault is usually theirs for not trying to make something of their opportunities. No moderator likes to force religion upon you. He can only advertise, encourage, and exhort; the participation is up to you. A spiritual activity will be successful if you, the students, make it so. If it fails, it is usually because you are not interested in the practical aspects of your Faith.

You, as a Catholic college student, must aspire to be a leader. You will have sufficient educational opportunities offered to you, and all the help necessary to advance yourself. What appears to be wanting among Catholics is the incentive, the motive force to overcome the inertia of their environment. In practice, the Catholic college graduate seems to adjust himself to the world instead of making the world adapt itself to the Faith and morality of the Catholic.

The last few popes have been insistent upon the need for the layman to recognize and practice the obligations of the lay apostolate which are his. Your four years of college will give you ample time and occasion to study this apostolate. The environment of the college should furnish you with motives to practice it. In these days of turmoil, suffering, militant atheism, and persecution there is little excuse for you to remain ignorant of your responsibilities and the means to actualize them. There is even less excuse for lethargy in the matter.

CHAPTER VI

Extra! Extra!
Extra-Curriculars!

→>>-→>>-→>>((-((-((

You have noticed, no doubt, that the most publicized aspect of college life is the extra-curricular. This is easy to understand because in addition to its being something entirely voluntary, there is also less routine, more variety and natural interest to it. Certainly a dance will hold the attention more readily than a class in mathematics. A game is more newsworthy than an examination. The extra-curriculars are an integral, vivid, and important part of the education of a college student.

Another factor in favor of the activities is that they give you a chance to put into practice many of the things you have learned in class. The college paper or magazine, for instance, can be a means by which the student will learn not only the art of modern writing, but also the craft of editing, layout, and various other technical skills required in journalism. International relations clubs, the different scientific clubs, debate clubs—these and others like them are the laboratories in which class matter is practiced in a more real and less scholastic atmosphere. The activities introduce into college life a small section of real life in which you may try yourself out to see whether you are improving. A student who does not get into at least one activity is missing an important adjunct to his college education.

There is, then, no question of the importance of these activities. The problem is how to use and not abuse them. Important as they are, they must not be permitted to interfere with your progress through the subjects in the regular curriculum. The course of studies is the real reason for the existence of the college, and it must always be given first place. Therefore, in determining which, and how many, extra-curricular activities you are going to enjoy, you must always bear in mind your ability to handle the curriculum itself so that you will not hamper your learning of class matter by too much enthusiasm for the activities. This is a problem in which your own judgment must guide you. It is better to be prudent in the beginning than to learn by healing the wounds of rough experience.

Sometimes the activities will stimulate your interest in your studies. From dramatics, for example, you can acquire a lasting interest in Shakespeare and other classics of the theatre. From political science clubs much of what would otherwise be "dry stuff" takes on a vivid immediacy as you see the abstract principles of the classroom being worked out among the nations, particularly within your own. Here we have one of the main reasons for extra-curriculars.

Again, through the medium of the activities, you meet many students whose names you would never have known otherwise. You learn not only their names, but all about them because there is no better way to know a person than by working with him. All of a man's strengths and weaknesses come to the surface when he is doing something which makes him forget to be self-conscious. Incidentally, you yourself, if you are plagued by too much self-consciousness, will find the activities a help in overcoming it.

The social whirl, too, has its place as an instrument for smoothing off the rough edges of your personality and polishing you up for the social relations of your life—relations which are necessary for everybody except a hermit. In this division of extra-curriculars you are in most danger of overdoing it. Preparing for dances and teas takes time; more time is required to participate; and still more time to clear things up afterward. These affairs have no connection with class work—that is why they are good recreation—and hence, as far as your studies are concerned, the time is lost. Be careful how much time you spend on them!

Dancing can be a way of making others happy. Apparently not all who go to dances go to dance. If one may judge by the number of students standing around supporting the walls, many merely pay for the tickets in order to watch the proceedings.

Granted, you cannot dance all the time, but the observer feels that much more dancing could be done than is the custom. Why the hesitancy? When you dance with a girl, you make no lifelong commitment. You do not have to marry the person you dance with. To ask a girl to dance with you is merely an attempt to help her to enjoy her evening. It should be the objective of every person present to dance as many numbers as he can. This could be a practice of the virtue of charity, with the added inducement of a supernaturally meritorious as well as enjoyable evening. The service of God and gaining of merit do not always consist in the performance of unpleasant duties.

One certain gain for all students who conduct or manage these activities is the deepening of their sense of responsibility. All need constant drill in this department of their personalities. If this were the only good done by extra-curriculars, it would justify their existence.

While we are on the subject, we cannot help but say a few words about courtesy. Crudeness is not a sign of masculinity, nor are good manners something you are born with—something attendant upon the simple act of growing up. They are the happy result which follows the long process of sanding down the rough edges of your personality. Your association with everybody, especially girls and older people, should be marked by courtesy and chivalry. Trifles count in this matter, and girls expect these little attentions. A habit of opening and closing car doors, calling at the front door of the girl's home rather than blowing the horn of the car to attract her attention, stepping aside for ladies to pass, and many other points of etiquette should be routine for a college man.

Nor is it a proof of your manhood to drink your way through a social event. It seems to be a mistaken notion that a preference for hard liquor is a masculine characteristic, whereas it is no more a sign of virility than taking medicine or having a tooth pulled. In fact, since liquor tends to befuddle the senses and weaken the use of the free will, drinking to excess is anything but manly; it is rather a weakness. The strength of will required to refuse a drink or to moderate your drinking is much more a sign of manhood, since you may have to overcome the jibes of the ever-present weaker characters.

The yearly round of proms, balls, and hops with their orchestras, vocalists, corsages, taxis, demands quite a treasury. You may be one of the fortunate students who does not need to think twice about spending money. Again, you may not. In either case, it would be good training for life to think seriously about all this expense, and to weigh the amount of real relaxation and pleasure obtained against the consequent financial strain. Perhaps your parents can afford this burden. Even so, if it is unnecessary, it is un-Christian, that is, a waste. If you are one of the larger number who cannot afford so much spending, the argument gains in weight. When the social whirl is the custom, the "thing-to-be-done," those who cannot afford it will sometimes force themselves into debt in order not to appear conspicuous.

All things considered, it may be better, sometimes, to "sit this one out," that is, to stay home and study. After all, that is the main work of college, and it is too easy to lose sight of the main issue amid the glitter of momentary pleasure.

CHAPTER VII

Rah! Rah! Rah!

≫≫-≫≫-≫≫-≪≪-≪≪-≪≪

THERE is no doubt that athletics do add glamor to the name of a college. There is nothing like success to draw attention and acclaim, and a winning college team is considered the height of success. Apart from the financial returns (in which you, as a student, will probably not be interested), it is pleasant to know, and have people recognize, that the name of your school is associated with glory on the field of combat. You, then, will be able to bask in the reflected light of this glory. You will have something to talk about between games, and each game will be something stimulating to look forward to.

But, let's be realistic! How many students participate personally in their school's intercollegiate athletic program? During your college career you will probably have nothing directly to do with the teams. Hence, as far as *your* education is concerned, intercollegiate athletics are useless! You cannot improve yourself, you know, through the victory of someone else. To be sure, athletics have a limited educational value—for the ones playing. But for you, shouting from the benches, the whole situation is vicarious.

One of the most immediate effects of participation in athletics is the training in discipline needed for teamwork. The development in self-control arising from it will, almost certainly, carry over into daily life. To forget yourself unselfishly in order to work toward the victory of the team engenders a very useful sense of perspective which is notably absent from the lives of many today. The athlete learns that the individual is seldom as important as the cause for which he is working. We might extend this idea further and say that life is very much like a game. Stars are indeed important, and all the members of the team must strive to become stars; however, the striving is not to be such that each will go his individual way at the expense of team play. All members must be welded into a unit in which their individual talents are worthwhile only inasmuch as they contribute to the success of the unit.

Unfortunately, you may be one of those unable to profit from participation in intercollegiate competition. Yet the case is not hopeless. There is a form of athletics open to every student in the college—the intramurals. In these sports you will find practically all the benefits to be gained from membership on the team without the agony of big-time competition. You will gain the recreational good, the training in self-control, the idea of teamwork, and the stimulation of the competitive spirit. Intramurals have now come to be recognized as part of the educational scene. If you are wise, you will play your share in them.

Athletics can be, and are, overemphasized. They even take up too much of the student's thinking time. Sport is recreation, and is to be only a part of one's life. The better part of your time should be spent in thinking of, and conversing about, serious things. The world today is burdened with many problems, and at graduation you will fall heir to them. While you have the time and opportunity, you should exercise yourself in pondering the state of society so that you may come forward later with your bit toward its Christianization.

A Catholic college will always remain an educational institution. No matter how thrilling the game of the day before, the prosaic business of class follows on the morrow. You must attend your lectures and pass your tests even though the team is in a distressing slump. The worth of the college depends on the ability of its faculty, not its team. You will be fortunate if you pick a school with a learned faculty, even though its teams may not be of the best. The learning of the professors does not fluctuate with the weather, the strength of the opposition, or the darkly surmised malfeasance of the referee. It is certainly pleasant to have a winning team, but it is not vital to your future.

Suppose you should, while in college, become a nationally known athlete. What will it profit you during the examination in epistemology? If your college is worth its salt, you will always be made to park your athletic reputation outside the classroom. A fast-breaking curve will not settle an argument in apologetics, nor will a 44-point average per game be the answer to a quadratic equation. Educationally, you win with your brains—not your brawn. Can you be sure that your athletic prowess of today will make you happy tomorrow? Will you be paid a salary in 1980 for having been a star in 1970? Only if you have a job as an athletic coach! You certainly cannot eat your clippings when you are hungry, nor will your devoted fans support you for life. Athletics have their place in college, but it is definitely circumscribed. The saga of the team is not the whole story.

CHAPTER VIII

The Old Alma Mater

≫≫-≫≫-≫≫≪≪-≪≪-≪≪

You will hear much in college about school spirit. In fact, you may often think you know what it means. Many of the gestures of college students, particularly the heroic and unusual, are attributable to it. For example, the athlete running himself breathless, the magazine editor working himself thin, the debaters studying long hours in the library to uphold the good name of the school on the platform—these and other newsworthy events are traditionally taken to be examples of school spirit. Now, we do not intend to cast the shadow of a doubt on the truth of this, yet, because such things are unusual (when the number of students doing them is compared with the total number), you are apt to get an entirely false impression of the essential meaning of school spirit.

At bottom, school spirit consists in making some kind of identification of yourself with the school. Once you are enrolled in college, this occurs almost automatically. You boast to your friends, "We won this game," or, "We have a fine dramatic society." The use of the *we* is an instinctive, implicit linking of fortunes with the school. Of course, you do not pretend to possess the college by way of complete ownership, but you feel that you and the administration have many things in common.

School spirit is essentially a jealous unity which develops between the student and the college community. You base your foundation for boasting upon the cooperation of the students in upholding the dignity of the school, and upon the unity of the president, dean, and faculty in exemplifying the standards of its tradition. All, students and faculty alike, are devoted, not to a mere abstraction, but to a living personality manifested in the community life of the whole group. On the part of the student, a loyalty grows which would make it unthinkable to be disloyal in any way. On the part of the school, the spirit is shown in a maternal interest in every venture of the students, no matter how trivial. The school rejoices with each of their successes, and mourns with their failures. When such a situation obtains, you can say, "Our school is great," because you, the students, are great.

The close bond which education forges between pupil and master is the basic reason for such a thing as school spirit. In the educational process something of the educator is given to the one being educated, so that there develops a kind of spiritual relationship between them. You rarely find this expressed in words of any kind, but it is none the less a fact. It is felt on both sides, and the normal type of student reacts to it.

It follows that if you have real school spirit, you

will always be ready to help a fellow student because you will sense the oneness which exists between you. You will never speak disparagingly of your school, your faculty, your fellow students. On the contrary, you will always be swift to advertise your school on every possible occasion. You will want others to share its advantages with you, and you will do all in your power to influence their joining you. If you have the proper school spirit, you will praise much (for there is always much to be praised); and you will complain little because, in the long run, there is little room for legitimate complaint in the average Catholic college. It is true that all human beings make mistakes, but you will overlook these if you are occupied in looking for all the good you can find. Do not be a chronic complainer; it is too easy and too common. It indicates a mind that is sliding down hill. It takes intelligence to praise; griping requires no brains.

Where genuine school spirit exists, it will appear in action; it will assume a tangible form in the deeds of the students. For example, where athletic contests draw the majority of the student body, where dramatics and debate never have to look for an audience, in a school where every page of the college paper attracts readers, there you may be sure that the spirit is flourishing.

Since the student council is the official voice of the students, a loyal student will know his class representatives and transact business with faculty and administration through them. Many times the school, or some committee of the school, will put on a drive for clothing or something else for the missions. The real student, because he has the good of the college at heart, will support all of these drives to the best of his ability. The school should be considered a second home, and anything which would disturb the order in his home will be noted and checked by the loyal student. This will call for occasional correction of other students, especially underclassmen, who forget themselves. It will also demand hard study to maintain high grades because your record is part of the school's record.

This may be a good place to say something to you about care for the physical set-up of the college. Children, they say, are destructive around the house. However, college is for the young adult, and young adults are not supposed to be characterized by destructiveness. The reason children are so destructive is that they do not have the intelligence to see the damage they are doing. The same excuse can hardly apply to college men. Since you are a part of the college and the college is a part of you, you should treat the buildings and grounds accordingly, keeping them neat and in as good repair as possible. Things do wear out, all too fast, but an adult is careful to slow down the wearing process. Lack of care for the physical plant will show results. The place will take on a careless and slovenly appearance and will thereby become a less pleasant place to attend. You should be proud of the beauty of your college buildings and of the campus—proud enough to feel a sense of responsibility for keeping them that way.

Finally, let us call to your attention your school's good name. After graduation, your name will be connected with it for life. The better the reputation of your school, the better it will be for you who carry it. A good name cannot be bought, nor can it be earned by advertising, nor by any easy method. It has to be lived before it will be recognized, and that takes time. Sad to relate, good reputations can be lost very quickly by the foolish actions of the unthinking few. Hence, remember that wherever you go, the name of your school goes with you. You are always from "such-and-such" a college, and, whatever you do, your college does through you. Remembrance of this responsibility and the attempt to be worthy of it will hasten your maturity.

CHAPTER IX

Browsing Around

-》》-》》-》》《-《《-《《

THE modern college library is more than a book garage. It is intended to be used for other things than the housing, hiring, and repair of the best that has been written. Anyone who goes to the library solely to borrow or return an educational assignment is about as practical as a man who will never eat in a restaurant, but always takes the food home with him. The library is the intellectual workshop of the campus wherein you, the student, can work out for yourself most of the ideas that have inspired you in the classroom. You may sum up the meaning of the library, therefore, by saying that it is the storehouse, the information center, the intellectual headquarters of the college.

Sometimes the library building is one of the finest in the college group. Gothic-towered it may be, with a bit of ivy clinging to the distinguished, well-cut stone, and, perhaps, even a stained-glass window or two will be there to add to the medieval charm. If I have just described your library, rejoice that your college has the wealth to give you such beautiful surroundings, for not every college has. Yet, although this beauty is inspiring, it is still not the library. To find that, you must pass through the doors, be they awe-inspiring or humble, and enter upon the world of books.

A book is one of the greatest (if not the greatest) inventions of human genius. It is the closest approximation to a human being that man can fashion entirely by himself. Yet, it is not human, it cannot change its mind, it does not become pig-headed and refuse to listen to you, but it merely tells its own story and, for better or for worse, sticks to it. Some books are clothed in shabby garments and seem to shuffle along with their hands in their pockets, their shoulders hunched against a disapproving world. Others are just the opposite, being forever decked in the splendor of full evening dress. Some volumes stand rigidly aloof in their sober academic garb; their purpose in life being serious, they will brook no nonsense. Nearby you may see the cheerful Bohemian with his bright colors and jaunty print. Oftentimes this fellow can be lots of fun, but do not be fooled by his slap-dash style; he may have plenty of solid stuff in him. Down the shelf a bit you will find a very different character. Merely by looking at him you can tell he is an authority. He has that deep look of abstraction as though he were brooding over thoughts within him which were much more absorbing than his student clientele.

This other section is reserved for the officials of the book world—the reference books. Some of them are large and ponderous, walking heavily, their pages crowded with matters of world-wide importance. Beside them are huddled the minor officials, battered and wearied in the faithful performance of their duties. They are always so busy they never have time to pause and refresh themselves with new bindings.

No, these books are not human, but they are the next thing to it. Each has its distinct personality; and when you find several by the same author, you may even notice personality differences among them, due to the author's varying moods as he wrote them. As is the case among human beings, so also among books. There are books for every mood, books with every degree of culture and learning; there are the flighty empty-heads, and there are the cryptic, enigmatic individuals which are exasperating puzzles, but fascinating, none the less. If you make the right friends among books, they can lead you on to unbelievable heights of ideal and achievement. Fall among bad company, and your life can be utterly ruined.

Now, it may be that you are not a good mixer. You may be the bashful type, and feel somewhat at a loss in this world society of books. We thought of that contingency, and we have supplied for it. Meet the hosts and hostesses of the book world— the librarians!

These quiet, soft-spoken people can be, if you will permit them, a very potent influence toward your education. Since they are specifically trained for their work, they are as capable as any other members of the faculty of assisting you to develop yourself in a way that will be of everlasting benefit to you. The reason they are not, so far, considered to be teachers is because of the narrow meaning custom gives the name *teacher,* and because our educational mores have not yet caught up with the idea of courses (for credit, to be sure!) in book handling, given by professional librarians, as an accepted part of every man's education. Because books are (theoretically, at least) so important to the progress of mankind, you would wonder how the educators could have overlooked the need for this study. Quite a profitable semester might be spent by a student in learning how a book is made, the type fonts, the influence of type-shape on book content, the printing and binding of books, the inner format, the making of an index, the layout of the chapters, how books are categorized and catalogued, the relative merits of the two main systems of call numbers—the Dewey Decimal and the Library of Congress systems—how to consult the catalogue, what important encyclopedias and reference books there are in every library, and a multitude of other library facts, all at present unknown to the average student. Until this course is a part of the regular curriculum, education in books will depend on the initiative of the individual student.

Let us, therefore, urge you, young man, to ask the help of the librarians in learning how to get all you can from the use of the library. They know many good books to recommend to you, and they can also guide you away from useless or bad books. You should ask them for reading lists on current topics not directly connected with your class matter. Pay attention to the exhibits they set up from time to time, as you may learn more this way than you think. In short, if your college has a library, don't be afraid to be seen in it frequently.

However, you may be one of those who find working in the library an utter impossibility. "Too much noise," may be your verdict, as it is of many serious students. Some have said that they would prefer to settle down comfortably to read in a nearby foundry, rather than try the reading room of the library. Harsh as this judgment seems, a little experience has convinced us that there is much truth in it. Yet, who is to blame? The students! You are the ones who make the noise that bothers you! You turn the place into a social club where conversation is more important than reading.

You may say that it is the other fellow who makes all the noise, and that you are blameless. Granting your claim, it is probably true that there are also others who feel the same way about it. Then, why do you not band together and use co-operative action on the offenders? You have the right to peaceful study hours in the library, and no one can reasonably object if you stand upon your rights. Here is an opportunity to do a bit of apostolic work: return the reading room into a reading room! First set the example yourself by never violating the traditional library rule of silence; then, invite others to join with you in this worthy cause; and, finally, if there are still some who prefer to be anarchists, bring pressure to bear upon them.

Yet, the rule of silence is not the only regulation of the library. There are also the rules concerning the length of time you may keep books out. Some are to be withdrawn for only a day at a time; others may be kept for a week; whereas the majority may be held for two weeks without penalty. Some may be renewed for an additional two weeks; others may not be renewed at all. There are, likewise, certain other books which may not be taken out, but are retained constantly on reference shelves. Frequently an instructor will give the librarian a list of books to be put on a shelf under his name or under the name of his course, in order that they may always be in the library to help his students with their assignments.

It goes without saying that you should make it a point of honor never to violate any of these rules. Since they are for the good of large numbers of students, it would be an act of utter selfishness for you to place your whims before the good of so many others. Learn at once what the regulations of your library are, for the withdrawal and return of books, and abide by them. You will be thanked by the whole student body.

"Of making many books there is no end" (Eccles. 12:12), says the Scripture. That observation was made many years ago, and think of the number of books published since! One of the things we *can* say in praise of modern times is that there are books in profusion produced on every topic under the sun at reasonable prices. Only a madman would die of thirst in the midst of this reservoir of knowledge. Yet, no college library will contain all the books in print, nor even all the books written on the subjects in the curricula offered in that college. This would be too costly and impractical an ideal. Usually a school library will have as its purpose to obtain all the necessary books, and, within its budget, all the best books on the pertinent subjects. If, therefore, there are books which you need to read, and they are not in your library, ask the librarian to borrow them for you from some other library. Almost all libraries now belong to an interchange system whereby, by a kind of "share the wealth" program, they help each other out. Take advantage of this means of wider reading and research.

It should be the ambition of every student eventually to have his own library, but to keep this within the family budget will take wise planning and choosing. It would be well, then, to make a start at it as soon as you enter college by keeping your textbooks and using them as a foundation for further development. Around them you can gradually collect a growing number of good books whose acquaintance you have made during your course. Titles will be suggested to you by bibliographies found in the textbooks, from incidental remarks made by your teachers, and from other books you have come across while tracking down references. The awareness that arises from a steadfast purpose will make you book-conscious and will lead you to many a find.

If you can develop a love for books and reading

during your college life, you will have gained much toward your future happiness. Books are important; they do not "just happen." They are the result of long, hard work by the author, publisher, designer, printer, binder, and sales force. When they finally reach the library, books are rather valuable objects—much more than their prices would indicate. No price tag can equate the cost in intelligence and skill put into the making of a book. You should treat them all as though they were very close friends.

And, as a final suggestion: since most college libraries are run on a rather tight budget, you students could make yourselves great benefactors of the college by each of you donating a book-a-year (new or second-hand, it wouldn't matter) to your library. A mathematical genius would not be needed to compute the magnificent total gift that would be!

CHAPTER X

Where Dwellest Thou?

->>>->>>->>><<<-<<<-<<<-

WHEN some students go to college, they really "go." They leave kith and kin, pack up, and go into a strange land. Having settled down, they proceed to make a new life for themselves. Living on campus can be intriguing to a young person, and you should, if it is possible for you, give some thought to it.

There are things to be said for and against boarding at college. Probably, like everything else in this world, evil or good will be gotten from the experience according to the degree of good will in the one experimenting. Those who oppose dormitory life will relate many a dark tale about college boarding students running wild in the excesses of their dissolute lives. Magazines and newspapers do nothing to correct these impressions by the way they play up the more lurid incidents of college campus life. We would be the last to deny the truth of what is reported, or that there is a certain risk involved in sending a young man away from home to make his own way. Yet, chances must be taken in this world. Even the great number of traffic accidents and deaths would hardly excuse from over-caution the parent who would forbid his children to leave the house for fear of their lives. All men are expected to take prudent chances, and sending a young man away to college is an instance in point.

With the venture, however, must go safeguards. Since a young man must sometime break away from his mother's apron strings, boarding at college would seem to be as safe a way of doing it as any. For the student of a Catholic boarding college will live in dormitory buildings under the watchful eye of "prefects," who are either priests, religious, or mature laymen, appointed to live with the students and act as their counselors and friends. The boarding student, then, is not entirely on his own, yet, he is sufficiently alone to enable him to grow gradually in self-sufficiency and responsibility. Since he will live in proximity to the priests of the college, he will have the opportunity of seeing and consulting them as frequently as he wishes.

It may come as a surprise that in Catholic colleges there is nothing resembling the fraternity house system. No matter what kind of boarding houses or dormitories are in use, living in them is not determined by "pledging," or by any other restrictive standards set up by students. Hence, where you live is not a reason for snobbish exclusiveness nor for intellectual pride. Whether you are an inmate of the "Alpha Beta Gamma Delta House" or the new "Southeast Building" will be due more to the year you are in, or the amount of money you wish to pay for your room, or to your taste in furnishings, than to any snob appeal you may have.

The average dormitory room in a Catholic college is arranged for study. Luxuriousness of quarters is not encouraged. Although the room is the place where the student lives, it must mirror the main purpose of his life. Hence, it will probably be a place conducive to study, with the desk a prominent landmark. Congenial roommates thus become important objectives of search. Finding them may require a little time and diplomatic conditioning, but any normal young man should be able to engineer it. All things considered, therefore, there should be more of an atmosphere of study in a college dormitory than in a private home.

Among the advantages of living on campus you must consider the stimulus of novelty. Sojourning among strangers adds to the impression of "getting a new start in life," and this often means much to the young. You will be among strangers, not one of whom knows your past mistakes and failings. You will have no prejudices to overcome, no mental blocks in your own mind. Even if you have made a fine reputation in high school, here in college you need not feel constrained to live up to it. Hence, the pressure on you is eased, leaving more nervous energy for new worlds to conquer.

Boarding keeps you in the atmosphere of the extra-curricular activities. Not having to travel every day to and from school, you may be tempted to enter more fully into the extra-curricular life of the school. This is not a mere surmise if we may judge by the number of boarders normally found in the activities. It is certainly a consideration worth weighing when trying to make up your mind whether or not to board. This fuller participation in the student community will contribute to the increase in the school spirit of the student, with the consequence of getting much more out of college life.

In spite of all this, gloomy forebodings will occur to the fond parents. Suppose he gets among bad companions! Suppose that, because of the absence of the stern parental eye, he does not make himself study! Suppose, in spite of faculty supervision, he wanders off the campus frequently! What will happen to him? These and like spectres will haunt the dreams of parents, no matter what. But it is best to be realistic and admit that such things could happen even at home. All children must be left to God and their guardian angels much of the time. God and the angels may be trusted!

CHAPTER XI

What Next?

➤➤➤➤➤➤➤➤➤➤➤➤➤➤➤

L EARNING is a lifetime job. You realize that more and more the older you grow. The more you come to admit it to yourself, the more you can be sure your education has taken effect. There are always new things to be learned; there are new ways of doing old things. In addition to the necessity of learning constantly in order to keep up with the world, there is also the advantage of being at ease among others of a similar fresh and youthful bent of mind.

As a person grows older, he tends to become "set" in his ways. He views his youthful past as the only safe, sound, good, wise, and everything-else-that-is-great time the earth has ever known. He also becomes timorous since he does not have the courage or energy to fight his way as he did when young. Hence, we notice the tendency of older people to reminisce, to hesitate, to condemn that which is new, to do nothing. It is important, then, not only for success in life, but also for personal satisfaction and intellectual enjoyment, to attempt to keep up with all the latest developments in whatever field you are engaged, and in as many other fields as is reasonably possible. This fends off stagnation of mind, obscurantism, and other evils of the intellect which not only hinder progress but also prevent personal success and destroy one's own happiness as well as that of others.

Informal education for the rest of one's life should be, then, the accepted thing for the college man. If you have used your college course to advantage, you will have acquired all the tools necessary to continue your education at home in the midst of your books. No one should leave his future to chance. Modern life is fiercely competitive, and to the victor go the spoils. From high school on, you should ponder what station in life you want to occupy, what career you wish to follow, and all your efforts should be channeled in that direction. Since you now have it in your power to determine largely what will be your life's occupation and preoccupations, you would be acting foolishly if you did not seize every opportunity to advance toward your goal.

In addition to careers in business, there are also many openings after college in the professional and graduate schools. Bona fide specialists are always in demand, and the graduate or professional school is the place where specialists are made. It is possible, nowadays, for you to specialize on the graduate level in practically anything. There is no reason why the Catholic college graduate should not share proportionately in this specialization.

We learn from published statistics that the Catholics of the United States form approximately one-fifth of the population. It is much to be doubted that they form one-fifth of the graduate or professional students in the country. There seems to be no valid reason why this should be.

If the objection is given that Catholics are proverbially from families in moderate circumstances, if not actually poor, there is an answer. There are so many fellowships, assistantships, scholarships, and the like, offered today in so many different fields that many of the so-called "poor Catholics" could easily be accommodated if they had the courage and ambition to work for these helps. We can grant you that at one time prejudice plus poverty were formidable obstacles for a Catholic to overcome. Today, neither of these amounts to a row of pins for a Catholic who has ambition and a normal amount of courage.

The graduate level of science and technology is the realm in which things are being done today. If Catholics are to live up to their obligations of being apostolic, of being the "leaven" which is to mix in until "all is leavened," then it is about time that Catholics took entry into graduate fields and professional schools as a matter of routine procedure. One suspects that more often than not laziness hides behind the cry of "poverty and prejudice." It takes work to become a specialist, to become a man who is a leader in his field. It takes long hours of work, and a lazy man does not like work.

There should be in every Catholic a spirit of adventure. His religion should inculcate that in him. A mere brief survey of a Catholic's beliefs is enough to indicate the sublime ideas and ideals and the universal sweep of the plan. The creation, the fall of the angels, earth the battleground on which Satan wars against God (with man in the middle), the Redemption as God's master counterstroke, the Church as the Mystical continuation of Christ upon earth, the fact that life is a calculated risk, with heaven and hell hanging in the balance as the only alternatives—this array of doctrines should instill into the Catholic a spirit of daring, of adventure, of high aims and ambitions, and hosts of other qualities which would augur success both in this life and in the next.

Of course, it is necessary for the Catholic to think of these things before he can be inspired by them. If his magnificent intellect and free will, given him by God, are totally occupied with money grubbing and casting about for the best type of "job" without any thought to the significance of the work, he never gives himself a chance to rise above the earth and material things.

Yet, the Catholic has the opportunity to follow a career which is far above anything this world has to offer. A vocation to the priesthood or the religious life, it is true, is a call from God, and only those may follow who have first been called. But the call of God is more frequent than you think. Many, like the rich young man, hear the invitation and do not accept—not because they have "great possessions," as he had, but for some equally invalid reason. They look upon the religious life as too hard, indeed, far beyond them, forgetting that they do not live it alone, but have the help of God. Others imagine that they are unable to give up their precious independence in the world, as though a layman, bound as he is to his spouse, his children, his job, the conventions of society, military service, and all the rest, has a life of untrammeled freedom!

A religious vocation is not a call to a life in which there are no troubles. Nor is it an invitation to enter heaven immediately after death, nor anything else equally ridiculous. The priest and the nun are not born to the life. Before they followed the call of Christ, they were perfectly normal human beings, indistinguishable from the majority of their classmates. Mysteriously, God chose them in preference to others. They acted with decision, and have continued to cooperate with the grace of God; that has made them what they are.

Nor must you think that because a vocation is a supernatural gift it is therefore given in a strange, unusual, and easily recognizable way. There are no heavenly voices, no excessively pious feelings, no perceptible sweetness and light required. For a vocation to be genuine the following conditions should be verified: 1. sufficient good health to be able to live the life; 2. a good moral character, vouched for by your confessor; 3. an intelligence capable of handling the studies required by the way of life proposed; 4. the desire and the decision to follow such a life.

The determination to go ahead with it, come

what may (after seeking the advice of a priest), is the surest sign that the vocation is a true one. Oddly enough, it is usually as prosaic as that! Anyone who delays his application until he is assured by some supernatural sign may continue to wait until it is too late.

From freshman year on, then, you should interest yourself in the possibilities that lie before you after college. Much time and money can be saved by giving yourself leeway for this. You have the opportunity to adapt your curriculum to your planned future. You can choose your electives with foresight. If you have a goal which lies beyond college, you will have more incentive to learn well while you are here. In brief, your attitude as a college man should be that, if you do not get into graduate or professional school, it will be because of some very cogent reason which weighs more in the eternal view.

PART II

The Philosophy

➤➤➤➤➤➤➤➤➤➤➤➤➤➤

CHAPTER XII

A Human Approach

>>>->>>->>>-<<<-<<<-<<<

N<small>O MATTER</small> what theory of education you hold, in the last analysis you must educate yourself. An excellent college with a national reputation and a faculty second to none in the country will avail nothing toward your education if you do not use your own will power to develop yourself. The teachers, the teaching methods, the textbooks, and the library are all very important, but you must want to profit by them if they are to be a profit to you.

You can be driven to school by various forms of coercion, but you cannot be made to think or reason. Until you begin to think, and to think for yourself, you are not showing the symptoms of an education, even though you may be memorizing and reciting facts by the book-full.

Even study, in itself, is not education. Study is a means, and an essential means, to an education, but normally study looks to but one aspect of the process, namely, the development of the intellect. Admittedly, this will be a very important factor in your total education, but there is more to it than that. If you are to be truly educated, not only your mind, but your complete human nature must receive adequate development.

Although study is only a means to an education, it is still so important that you should pay careful attention to it so as to learn the proper study methods. Yet, even then, you will not employ these study methods with full effectiveness unless you have a philosophy of education to direct you. A successful study technique cannot be devised without a philosophy as its basis, but not everyone who follows the technique will perceive its philosophy. Up to the present, your philosophy of education has probably been unformulated, since you are too young and inexperienced to have thought it out. If you have cooperated with the Catholic schools which you have attended, your philosophy of education has been fundamentally that of Catholicism, even though you did not think of it as such. Following the correct philosophy blindly is better than following a false one, yet your education will mean more to you and have deeper and more lasting effects on you the more clearly you perceive the philosophy which inspires it. You will go ahead more rapidly and more successfully if you know where you are going and why. Our purpose, therefore, is to make explicit for you a sound philosophy of education in order that you may profit to the fullest from your college career.

On the supposition that education is a total development of the whole man, you will be educated when you are as fully developed as it is possible for *you* to be, and in as many ways as *you* are personally capable. There is no place for a relative view here. You are not well educated merely because you stand at the head of the class. You are well educated when you are as completely developed as *you* can be. Consequently, you will notice how it is possible for many men to go through life more or less uneducated, even though they are college graduates, because they did not get all they could out of college. Furthermore, the fact that two or more men have passed through the same curriculum achieving the same grades does not prove that they are equally educated. On the contrary, it is more than likely that they are not equally educated in view of the variety of talent and achievement usually found among young men. Education is so personal that it cannot be successfully conducted on a mass basis, unless each student can be depended upon to be trying his best at all times. The safest thing, then, is for each student to receive as much personal attention as possible in order that he may receive the greatest possible stimulation.

Another point worth stressing is that education must develop you progressively as a whole. It must not concentrate on your mind now, and then your body, but on the substantial union of body and soul together at all times. When your soul is the principal object, the body must not be forgotten; and when the body has its turn, the soul must be cared for too. It follows that even when you are engaged in athletics, or in some other form of physical training, you must act as a man, and not as a mere physical machine. Physical exercise should be taken in a way subordinate to the spiritual nature of man.

It was because it cared for this unchanging nature of man that the old-fashioned liberal education was as successful as it was. In the course of time it fell from favor, because of the immense scientific and technological advances. It was no longer thought to be preparing young people for life. Systems that were believed to be more efficient supplanted it, and they came in such profusion that the result has become no system at all.

Now, the efficiency of any given educational method will depend upon the way the means are used to effect the desired end. The means to an end may vary legitimately from time to time, according as changing circumstances make them now more, now less, effective. Although the end does not justify the means, it certainly has something to say about their practicability. Justification of means is a moral question; practicability of means is an intellectual one.

Accordingly, what you study in order to acquire an education is not nearly as important as how you study it. Language study, for example, was supposed to be one of the standbys of the liberal education, and yet, languages can be learned in a mechanical, lifeless way which has practically no educational value. On the other hand, accounting, considered a purely vocational subject, may be learned in such a human way as to have a very respectable educational value. For instance, if while you study it, you pay attention to the history of accounting, the ways in which the various systems evolved, and why one system seems to be better than another, you are putting yourself in contact with the human side of the subject. While learning a skill, you are developing as a man.

You must not forget this during your course of studies. As long as a subject in the curriculum has any reference to human beings, it has a human side, and should be approached from that side. In the concrete, the approach will consist in asking yourself "Why?" frequently. "Why do they do this? Why do they do it this way? Why is this way better than that? What is the significance of all this? If this were to disappear from the earth, what difference would it make in the lives of men?" If you study and learn in this manner, you will be educating yourself.

But in order to educate yourself with a maximum of efficiency, you should understand something of the nature of your being. What sort of person are you attempting to remake when you strive to educate yourself? What are your educational needs, your weaknesses, your abilities? What are the areas of your nature which must be cultivated if there is to be a total development of the whole man?

Upon analysis, you will find that you have six basic activities, or, to put it another way, you respond to life in a six-fold manner. Anything you say, do, or think will be included under one or several of these, so that if your education concentrates on all of them it will be a true education, a total development of the whole man. Conversely, if you bypass any of these areas while educating yourself, or if you neglect any part of any one of them, your education will suffer in proportion to the omission. You will, in that much, be uneducated. We may describe the six areas as follows:

1. *Impression.* The activity of the five senses, through which a man receives all his information naturally in this world.

2. *Expression.* A man's power to communicate, and his acts of communication with the outside world.

3. *Thought.* The activity which takes place within the mind of a man upon all the information received through the five senses.

4. *Religion.* The acknowledgment and acceptance of the Creator-creature relationship, and the actions consequent upon it.

5. *Aesthetics.* The power of perceiving, and the perception of the beautiful, over and above the good, the true, and the useful, together with the actions which follow from it.

6. *Discipline.* The control and guidance of the whole human being, either from within or from without, carried on according to the laws of God and man.

The next six chapters will contain a detailed study of each of the above areas, with the purpose of making clear its function in your education. To attempt to show how all the subjects of the curriculum apply to these areas would be too extensive an undertaking for our present discussion. Here is the place where you must do something for yourself. We would suggest that something like the following scheme might work out very well for you.

Take each of the subjects in your present curriculum, for example: English, religion, American History, mathematics, and French. Examine them, one by one, asking yourself these pertinent questions: 1. How do these subjects develop my powers of receiving information through my five senses? 2. How do they train me to express myself effectively? 3. In what way is my ability to think made deeper and keener by them? 4. What is their capacity to stimulate my relationship with God, both in understanding and in practice? 5. Do these subjects awaken my sense of the beautiful, arouse ideals, and spur me to productivity? 6. What effect do they have on my self-control, both personal and social?

If you are painstaking in this analysis, you will gradually discover the weaknesses in your study techniques, and you will find opening up for you new ways of getting more and more out of even the most conventional and (you would say) the dullest subjects. It will gradually occur to you that perhaps it is not so much your subjects as you yourself who are to blame for your not becoming a highly educated person. It will at least give a thoughtful student much food for serious thinking.

CHAPTER XIII

Receiving Impressions

->>>->>>->>>(((-(((-(((

THERE is nothing in your mind which has not come to you through your senses. There is no such thing as an innate idea. The importance of training the senses well should appear from this, that they are the gateways through which knowledge, useful and harmful, enters your mind. For this reason, not everything in the visible world should be permitted entrance. If you are to develop in harmony with the law of God, you must be careful that what you assimilate does not work to your downfall. An important part of your education, then, will consist in training your mind to select and reject from all the possible sources of knowledge that which will be most conducive to your greatest advancement in this world consonant with the glory of God, and to your salvation in the next.

In addition to the negative training of the senses, by which they are taught to reject that which will be harmful, education must also provide help toward their constant stimulation in the direction of always seeking that which will be most helpful.

It is easy, all too easy, for passion and prejudice so to blind you that much of what will be useful is not perceived. For example, it is notorious that you young people are headstrong: you cannot be told anything; you rebel against any sort of restraint. It is not that you really think you know everything. You know right well that you do not, but your pride fumes up and tells you that you will be acting in a weak and cowardly way if you permit yourselves to be led around by the nose. Hence, feeling that you must begin to stand on your own two feet, you rashly reject all advice and help. That is why most of you are hurt in your youth and live to regret it thereafter.

Even apart from the realm of morality you have a way of becoming blind to whole fields of knowledge so that your attention is restricted to specific, predetermined paths. For instance, having decided that you want to become a businessman, you may foolishly close your mind to the benefits of the study of literature, language, history, and other valuable subjects.

You must try to be more objective about yourself. Be humble enough to admit that you do not know much about the processes or the problems of education. Convince yourself that others who have succeeded will be able to lighten your burdens and ensure your success. In short, you must make yourself teachable if you are to educate yourself.

There are various channels through which sense impressions reach your mind. Reading is one of the most common, and, therefore, one of the most important ways in which the outside thought-world makes contact with you. (Notice, it is the first of the three R's!) Listening is another sense action which is employed almost constantly. Both of these must be objects of training in formal education and, indeed, in the old days, were trained with a severity worthy of their importance.

There are three other ways in which your sense impressions may be registered, namely, feeling, taste, and smell. These are considered inferior senses, not because they are unimportant, but because they are less directly connected with the mind. They are primarily physical acts, reductively intellectual. Hence, we call them inferior, but not unimportant. You need to have your senses of touch, taste, and smell trained with as much, and perhaps even more, rigor than the other avenues of learning.

There is still another channel which, because it is the work of all five senses together, is highly important and complex. Let us call it *observation*. By this we mean the constant attention, conscious or unconscious, which you pay to everything throughout your entire day. You probably do not notice the observing you do. That is because it is as natural as breathing. Just as you rarely think of how you breathe, and can, therefore, contract breathing habits injurious to your health, so, too, you can contract habits of observation injurious to your intellectual and moral health. Your powers of observation also need training.

Without further delay, let us examine the five

senses in turn, in order to understand their importance to your education.

A. READING

There are two phases to the art of reading: a. the mechanical skill by which you reproduce the printed page accurately within your own mind, or externally in sound waves, and b. the intellectual skill by which you interpret that which is represented on the page in arbitrary symbols called words.

Let us discuss the mechanical skill first. The following important qualities must be acquired:

1. *Accuracy*. Good vision and close attention are essential for accuracy. Your eyes must be good enough to see exactly what is written, or else you must be fitted with glasses. The discouragement to the learner, and the harm to education, caused by faulty eyesight put this matter beyond all argument. Close attention is equally important. That you can look at a thing without seeing it is a matter of daily experience; sometimes you even see something else in its place.

2. *Speed*. For proficiency in learning a fair amount of reading speed is important. If you are a slow reader, you can become more and more discouraged the further you go because there is so much extra reading to be done and, apparently, so little time to do it. But, for this speed you must not sacrifice accuracy. Your reading must never degenerate into mere page scanning

if you wish it to make a lasting impression on your mind.

3. *Interpretation.* By voice inflection, grouping of words and significant pauses, you interpret the author's complete meaning for yourself and, if you are reading aloud, for your listeners. This is indeed a most important achievement. It gives you much pleasure, while at the same time giving the author a fair chance by conveying his spirit and personality.

These are the three most important skills in the art of reading which you should bring to a point of proficiency. As we said, they are but mechanical. To support them you must deepen and strengthen your grasp of the following intellectual powers:

1. *Knowledge of words.* It goes without saying that a good vocabulary is indispensable in reading. If you do not have a thorough understanding of words, you will not be able to follow your textbooks. The accumulation of a sound working supply of words is not something which just occurs. It is the result of a deliberate program of the steady reading of good books, the use of a dictionary on words of whose meaning you are uncertain, and attempting to use these newly found words in your speech and writing. You should not leave the building of a vocabulary to chance.

2. *Knowledge of syntax.* Rules of grammar and syntax may be a torture to young students, but

they are not an idle affectation. Without them the art of communication would degenerate into a mere sharing of grunted elementary ideas. They are the tools of the cultured. The greater your mastery of them, the more subtle and deep will be your appreciation of the expression of others. Because you do not have a firm grasp of syntax, you may possibly miss the entire drift of an author's thought. There is question here of the effectiveness of your study.

3. *Understanding the whole.* While reading, it is not only necessary to understand what you read, word for word, sentence by sentence, paragraph after paragraph, but you must also comprehend the development of the entire work. In prose composition, a paragraph does not end the matter. Paragraphs are made to be linked to other paragraphs, until the chapter, the essay, or the book is complete. A chapter, essay, or book is much more than the sum of its paragraphs. Strive always for a sense of wholeness in what you read in order that the completed thought of the author may appear. Learn to think beyond the meaning of the sentence immediately before your eyes.

4. *Attention to implications.* This is another name for reading between the lines. Any written work worthy of more than superficial reading leaves much to the imagination and intelligence of the reader. This is not only legitimate, but stimulating. It will be a weary world when,

in order that the reader may follow, every last "i" must be dotted and every final "t" crossed. It is part of the pleasure of reading to take the author's words and transfer them, with the aid of his hints, into your own understanding of what he has said. To understand what this can mean, it is but necessary to read a book and then watch a film based upon it. You will quickly see how much your interpretation differs from that of the scenarist.

B. LISTENING

As in the preceding section on reading we stressed the need for good vision, so here we must not fail to mention the importance of the faculty of hearing. You should take care of your sense of hearing because impairment of it will handicap your education, not to mention the loss it causes in depriving you of the sound of music and the human voice.

In addition to the mechanical act of hearing, there is the psychological faculty to be considered. You must learn to hear not only what the other person says, but also what he implies. As there are tones, so, too, there are overtones which you must catch if you are to get the whole message. Some of the most delightful experiences of conversation are found in listening beyond the meaning of the word. It is done by being alert to the faint intonations given by the speaker.

Quite the reverse of the above is psychological deafness. You are thus afflicted when you hear not what is said, but only what you want to hear. It is very easy to become a victim of this infirmity. You suffer from it when you have a screen of your own preconceived ideas between your ears and your brain, so that sound from the outside world reaches you filtered of its harsh reality. It thus falls gently upon your sensitive feelings without disturbing your serenity. All is peaceful until you waken to the fact that education is impossible in that condition. Then, honesty may rally to your protection, but it cannot win without a bitter struggle. You must train your ears to be unaffected by your heart if their owner is to be an educated man.

Listening with intelligence to the words of others, especially if they be of some length, is a specialized art. Anyone can hear the words as they come from the mouth of the speaker, but not all will remember what he said two sentences ago, and only a select few will be able to give you a careful analysis of the entire speech when it is ended. Your ability to profit from classroom lectures is in question here and, if only for that reason, it should be a matter of vital interest to you.

In order to increase in listening efficiency, you must first pay careful and deliberate attention at all times. Second, exert constant mental effort to link sentence to sentence, and thought to thought. Third, create the knack of making a series of lightning reviews as the lecture progresses in order not to forget what has gone before. This will join the topics with each other in succession, and give you a frame of mind for receiving what is to follow.

Skill in listening to lectures is not easily acquired; but once you have it, you will see that it is well worth the effort spent in its attainment.

C. FEELING

This is the activity of the sense of touch, which, although not one of the nobler senses, is very important in your education. When trained properly, it can, through mortification and self-denial, help raise you to a high level of culture. If left untrained, it will drag you to the depths. For, among the animals the instincts given by God to control their lives are strong and well regulated; but, in you, reason takes the place of instinct, and if it shirks its job, your animal nature will run wild.

You, in common with most other men, will admit that you do not like rough treatment for your body. When left to yourself, you usually look for softness, ease, and pleasant sensations. In itself, this is not morally wrong, but it is a foolish attitude to take because, no matter how hard you try, you will be unable to avoid harsh experiences in this world. They will find you out in spite of your running away from them. Now, if you have not trained yourself to "rough it," you will, when finally brought face to face with the unpleasant side of life, react in a manner unworthy of your profession of Faith. During the course of your education, and throughout your life, never forget that you profess to follow Christ who led a stern life and died a hard death. You will be expected to live up to the standard of the Leader you follow.

We stress this part of your education because its importance, *as education,* is rarely discussed. Most people face the bitterness and roughness of life in a haphazard way, always hoping for the best and never foreseeing the worst; whereas, if they would consciously admit to themselves life's brutality, and systematically toughen themselves for its impact, fewer would surrender before it. If this seems like a grim doctrine, read the sayings of the wise men of history.

For life is a challenge, and all must meet it. Some will cringe away from it and go down to defeat; others will stand their ground, take the punishment that circumstances force upon them, and even seem to be overcome. But, physical suffering, even to the point of death, never denotes failure. The miseries of the sense of touch remain on the surface of the person unless he permits them to take over his entire self. He loses who quits, and, at this game, you cannot lose unless you quit.

Probably arising from physical softness is the habit of irresolution. You will often find yourself faced with a choice between two thorny paths, so that, no matter which one you choose, you will run into trouble. If you are not used to grappling with hardship wherever you find it, the difficulties of the choice will loom out of all proportion because you will see that, whatever your choice, you will have difficulty. Your instinct will be to run from making the decision, and you will try to get others to make up your mind for you. You will prefer that to thinking your own way to a conclusion and taking the consequences because you will then be able to blame others for whatever happens.

You will have many opportunities, during your college career, to educate your body to tough living, and your soul to hard and honest thinking. If you attempt to avoid all effort and to get away with as many things as you can, you may, during your school days, succeed—after a fashion. But life will eventually catch up with you, and the showdown will be the harder to bear the longer it has been delayed. Since a scholarly life has an asceticism all its own, a soft physique is not congenial to it. If the body has not been toughened, the soul will have less chance to work out its destiny.

D. SMELLING AND TASTING

Because these two senses are very closely related, we shall consider them at the same time. The method of educating them consists mostly in a course of self-denial, that is, in refusing to yield, or even pay attention, to their sensuous urgings and fastidious repugnances. They are instinctively attracted to that which is most fine and delicate, and are repelled by the coarser elements of life. There is nothing intrinsically wrong in this, but when you remember that you are a victim of original sin and that one of your deadly enemies is the concupiscence of the flesh, it is not hard to see how these two senses could easily betray you into the hands of the enemy. It is imperative for you to remember that control of these senses cannot be had for the asking. You must be constantly vigilant, building up within yourself a strong indifference to their objects.

E. OBSERVATION

As long as you are awake, you are observing. If you have the use of your senses, it is impossible for you not to notice things. You make mental note of the changing of light and shadow, the passage of solid objects before your eyes, the sound of human voices, the sensation of the physical impact of foot on pavement or hand in water. The acrid smell of smoke annoys you; you enjoy the taste of a good dinner. Because of the report of your senses, you like some places and do not like others; some persons you "take to," others you avoid; you drink this rather than that; you prefer a sonata to a jig. Note that the majority of these observations are the work of a combination of senses helped by the reason. Since the average person falls into these likes and dislikes without realizing it, we may conclude that you are controlled, at least in part, by your environment.

Some of the impressions gained through the senses are weak; others are strong. It is the work of education to strengthen the weak, if they are worth having, and to weaken or eliminate the strong, if they are harmful. To put it more positively, you must train yourself to make a selection of impressions according to their usefulness or moral worth. It is impossible fully to eliminate or ignore all bad sense impressions. Some of them will intrude themselves upon the mind no matter what you do.

An educated man will see to it that as few as possible bother him, by training his mind to divert itself at once from the evil or useless, and to turn itself to that which is good.

The same thought may be expressed in a different way by saying that you cannot help having sense impressions, but you do not have to register them. To retain an impression, you must pay attention to it. As a rule, you see the scenery as it passes before your eyes, but you do not pay close attention to it unless you have a definite reason, such as finding your way about in a strange place.

With regard to other persons, unless you are dealing with them personally, there is no reason for paying more attention to them than you would to the scenery. In personal relations with people, however, it is good to use all the powers of observation possible. The more of their personal traits you note, the more sensitive you are to their tone of voice and changes of expression, the better able will you be to get along with them.

F. CONCLUSION

From our analysis of impression, you may judge how important it is in your education. From the beginning of your life, your whole approach to this world and the next will be colored by the knowledge and advice taken in by your senses. The grave obligation you are under to feed these senses with the right material and to prevent, at all costs, harmful matter from reaching you through them should need no more emphasis.

You have the serious duty to cooperate at all times with the educational forces which are attempting to fashion your life. Not only must you learn to use your senses properly in moral matters, but you must also strive always to perfect yourself in secular and temporal affairs by the diligent use of those same avenues of learning. Only under such circumstances will you be able to boast that you are receiving an education.

CHAPTER XIV

Expressing Oneself

->>>->>>->>>|<<<-<<<-<<<-

You are not self-sufficient; no one person is, nor will anyone ever be. Human beings need one another. The need arises in the helplessness of babyhood; it remains with you even in the prime of life when, in order to live, you must receive a salary from others; and it clings until the day you draw your last breath and others bury you. Your specific needs existing at any one time, their urgency and extent, must be communicated to others. The more perfect your self-expression, the better opportunities you give yourself. From the social nature of man we argue to the supreme importance of self-expression.

Human interdependence lays the foundation for two of the great virtues—justice and charity. Although they are virtues of self-expression, they demand that you recognize the existence, rights, and needs of others, and express yourself as befits the situation. Communicating with your neighbor is not at all a one-sided affair. He must be approached now one way, now another, and sometimes be left alone. His personal preferences must often be consulted. If he has set down any rules for making contact with him, you must honor them scrupulously if you wish to avoid barbarity.

From your side of the picture another set of considerations arises. In your transactions with others you may speak courteously or you may snarl; you may write satire or you may write a letter of condolence; you may rise to give someone your seat or you may knock someone down in order to go through a door first. These are all recognizable modes of self-expression. Some may enhance your glory, here and hereafter; others will tell people just what you are; still others can prevent your ever attaining a position of eminence.

There is no effort to communicate with another which does not have a two-fold effect: it strives to attain an objective, and it gives another a description of yourself. If you were to write a novel, it would tell one story about your characters and another about you. In delivering a speech, you may not be persuasive but you certainly are self-revealing. Even if you are too shy to speak in public when called upon, your refusal will nevertheless convey your own feeling of inadequacy. Self-expression must, therefore, be developed to whatever extent you are capable, unless you wish to be pitied as a social misfit.

To be done efficiently, the training of a person in expression must be broken down into stages. Written expression will be taken first, then oral, then, finally, some other methods which are less notable but very important.

This second of the three R's may be approached from the viewpoint of either the craftsman or the stylist. Taking the work of the craftsman first, let us say that he who would master the writing craft must be at home with words, sentences, paragraphs, whole compositions, and verse.

1. *Words.* It is of great importance for the student to be able to spell correctly if he is to give an impression of intelligence. We all joke about misspelled words but, even so, the judgment of an employer as well as that of a teacher will be swayed adversely by the sight of errors in spelling.

Penmanship also has its importance in the matter of written expression. Making people like and respect you is half the battle of influencing them, and, as we have said, to influence others is the purpose of self-expression. If your handwriting is clear and firm so that the readers do not have to struggle to decipher it, they will think that much more of you and will be the more easily persuaded by what you write.

Vocabulary in general was treated under impression. Here we have but to point out that the supply of words needed for expression is a "recall" vocabulary, that is, words which you can call up for use at will. It is more difficult to accumulate words of this kind. Their number will always be less than that of your "recognition" vocabulary, that is, those words which you understand when you meet them in a book, but which you do not know well enough to summon up at will.

2. *Sentences.* You should always check to be sure that you are writing in complete sentences, with subject, object and verb where they belong. There should never be disagreement between subject and verb, and the modifiers should be attached to the correct words. This may seem to be offensively elementary advice, yet, a glance at the average examination book or written student paper will reveal a surprising number of mistakes. They are probably due to carelessness, but an educated man is not careless.

3. *Paragraphs.* Although in modern prose style the paragraph is short and very pointed, it must contain a unified series of thoughts developed about a single theme. When you write, take care that your paragraphs are units with a limited but completed message. Do not drag them out unduly, nor yet cut them too short.

4. *Whole compositions.* Every educated man, even though he may not intend to become a professional writer, should be able to write complete compositions of considerable length. In adult life there will be various forms of written composition in constant demand: briefs, reports, business and social letters, even occasional speeches. To be effective, all of these must flow from a fair mastery of the art of composition. You must learn for life how to construct a solid,

unified, satisfying composition which will treat adequately all the facets of its main topic.

5. *Verse*. The composition of verse is a splendid exercise in written expression. You need not suffer the slightest bit of poetic frenzy or inspiration to succeed at it. It will suffice for you to apply yourself steadily to the rules, wasting no words, and being exactly sure of the meaning of every word you use. Your expression must be condensed, imaginative, and emotional, and yet, emotional in a way that is not sentimental or frothy. The rigid forms of metre and rhyme will develop in you an appreciation of economy and a sense of rhythm and music in language. The total effect of the practice of versification is usually a style which is clear, direct, terse and vivid.

In addition to the mechanical aspect of written expression, there is another which we may call intellectual. We call it this because this part of writing looks more to the thought development of composition and less to its external form. Yet, as must all communication, it will depend for its final impact on external expression.

1. *Clearness*. If you wish to express yourself clearly, you must force yourself to think clearly. Clear thinking is not as easy as it sounds. You must take your time, be patient, and have the courage to forego pet ideas and favorite expressions if you wish to come to the full truth. It would be worth your while to develop a habit-

ual suspicion of emotional influence. This can be accomplished very efficiently by the practice of putting your thoughts down on paper. Cold print has a dampening effect on the ardors of emotion. You might utter a sentiment orally and notice nothing wrong with it, yet seeing it in writing may convince you of its fatuity. The real test, therefore, of clarity and precision is to expose your thought to view on paper.

2. *Force*. Being clear is only part of the battle, for it is possible to be clear and dead. You may explain a point with the most translucent clarity, yet influence no one. Since the object of written communication is to change minds, at least to the extent of giving them new ideas or overcoming the inertia of their old ones, you will have failed in your purpose if you have been clear but not persuasive. Even in a personal letter you will have the desire to impress your friends by the thoughts you communicate to them. Your written expression must, therefore, have a force which develops from the truth vividly conceived and portrayed.

3. *Interest*. Interested people are interesting. If you care nothing for your subject, you will have difficulty in interesting others in it. Your own sincere conviction as to the worth of your writing is the thing which will enliven it. Even though you may be unconscious of its influence on your style, your personality has a way of manifesting itself through your writing. On the

other hand, there are many who never seem to take a subject to their hearts. These students learn easily, but their learning is done with such academic aloofness that they ignore all the practical implications of the material. They will study and master sociology from a textbook, never realizing that there are people living in their own city whose lives are made miserable by just such conditions as the students have memorized from the text. Their ideas seem to have no significance for them beyond the realm of their own minds. Written expression, to be interesting, dare not suffer from this woodenness, but must be alive with the author's convictions.

4. *Attractiveness.* The aesthetics of writing is almost beyond the possibility of accurate description or explanation. Attractive writing is, in the last analysis, a combination of many small details. Call it personality in writing, if you will. Attribute it to an artlessness of expression which conceals consummate art. You must anticipate the labor attendant upon the painstaking pursuit of the ideal, if you would write attractively, and the ideal is the perfect representation of the impression the author wishes to convey. To achieve this, you must have historical accuracy, thorough analyses, perspective, atmosphere, proper word shadings, order, neatness of detail, and proportion of parts. To sum up, attractive-

ness in writing is a combination of all the good qualities of the author, his subject, and his skill.

Needless to say, you will not acquire these qualities of a stylist without much hard practice. Once acquired, however, they will assure the effectiveness of your written expression. In this next section, we shall treat of speech, a department of life noticeable today more for quantity than for quality.

B. SPEECH

Many of the rules which we have applied to writing apply equally to speech. Such, for example, are knowledge of words, use of sentences, unity of topic, clearness. In this section we shall not repeat those instructions since you may easily reapply them to the present subject. Instead, we shall confine ourselves to advice which is specifically directed to the development of your oral expression.

When a person speaks, he communicates even more of himself than he does in writing. The reason is that speech goes forth in a sound which is peculiarly a part of the speaker. No one can ever reproduce exactly the sound of another's voice, because the voice has its own qualities which are determined by a man's physical makeup, his state of health, his disposition. Therefore, you should cultivate the faculty of speech in order to control the impression others receive when you speak.

Some people have flat, expressionless voices which communicate nothing beyond the mere meaning of the words themselves. Others are so gifted either by nature or by training that they can communicate whole paragraphs by the tone of voice alone. An interesting experiment would be to see how many different meanings could be conveyed by the simple word *yes*. It is possible to express surprise, hope, exasperation, weary patience, or anxiety, through the intonation of this one word.

You should never underestimate the effectiveness of the tone of your voice. An impressive delivery is ordinarily not a natural development ascribable to the maturing of the individual. Good speech comes from practice. If you would improve your speech, you must exercise yourself in placing and deepening it. You should seize every opportunity during classroom recitations to speak out firmly, crisply, and with the intention of speaking in public. If possible you should "aim" your voice not only at the instructor, but toward the student farthest from you in the room. Watch the effect it has upon him, and judge the results by his reactions. Proper modulation of voice comes from control of breathing, which, again, is obtained only through practice.

Finally, it can be taken for granted that you should attempt to make your pronunciation and enunciation as perfect as possible. Unless you become reasonably accurate in these matters, you will at least distract, if not annoy your listeners. Proper pronunciation consists in giving a word its correct accent. Clear enunciation consists in permitting every part of every word to be heard without exaggeration. These two qualities, plus a pleasant tone, are invaluable assets in business and in society.

One might surmise that speech and writing make up the whole of human expression, but such is not the case. There are other ways of transmitting and enhancing ideas. Their methods are more subtle, but an educated man should have some control of them. We mean your physical appearance and the gestures of your entire body.

The use of facial muscles has more than a little to do with the meaning of words. The proof of this may be gathered from watching a clever actor portray his part. He is never dead-pan unless his lines call for it. He makes use of eyebrows, eyes, mannerisms, shoulders, and hands, in order to convey with fullest force his meaning. Because he is on the stage, he uses these gestures in an exaggerated manner, but—and this is the point—he makes effective use of them. Without being theatrical, you should learn how to use, in moderation, all these aids to expression. They will be of immense help in making your way in the world, and, incidentally, they will make you a fascinating person.

One further word about self-expression: body control is important, too, especially in public appearances. A speaker who is ill at ease, stiff, or trembling can infect his audience with these same quavers, since such feelings easily communicate themselves. You will show that you are profiting by your education if you manifest sufficient self-control to speak in public with reasonable ease, if not with eloquence.

CHAPTER XV

The Thought World

-»»-»»-»»«-««-««-

WHEN you think, you are performing an almost purely spiritual action. We say *almost* because, as long as you remain a man, you will never be able to ignore the material part of your nature completely. Your imagination, which supplies the sounds and pictures for your thinking, is a material faculty, as are also your sensitive memory and your emotions. They need to be educated as well as the rest of you, but at present we are talking about processes which lie even deeper.

No one on this earth can perceive, with any hope of certitude, exactly what I am thinking, what pictures are in my mind, what emotions are stirring me. Furthermore, it is a rare person who comes to know me so well that he can make a good guess at them. Here, the individual is alone and is either the master or the slave of his lower nature. Yet, this deep, inner citadel must be reached by education. In fact, it is the most important target in the whole educational procedure.

But, to develop your thinking power is a most difficult task. You must be willing to open your mind and permit good educational influences to enter, at the same time guarding against the intrusion of evil. This calls for a precise balance between self-sufficiency and gullibility.

In order for your thinking power to be educated, you must desire that it be educated and you must cooperate with the work as fully as you can. Inasmuch as you rebel, in so much will your education cease. If you ask to have your thinking educated, you must anticipate hard and sometimes distressing application to your own training. If your ability to think is to grow, you are destined to suffer the growing pains of thought. From the outside only the most general kind of help will reach you. You must dispose yourself to take the help which comes from teachers, books, and experience, and use it again and again until you are master of your mind.

A. REASON

The essence of thinking is the perception of relations. We ordinarily call this the formation of judgments, i.e., taking two concepts (or ideas) and asserting the relationship between them. The more relations you can perceive, the more you can think. The key to education in reasoning or thinking, therefore, is to build up within yourself the raw material of relationships, the while you increase in the use of them. For example, let us take the concepts "man" and "good." Here we have material out of which to build at least two relations —"man is good" and "man is not good." If, as a beginner, you were to limit yourself to those two ideas, your thinking would indeed be meager. Since you could not form many relations, you would be hampered in the further acquisition of knowledge. Hence, the faculty of reasoning needs a supply of ideas with which to work, and the owner of the faculty must be versatile in using them—transposing them and forming more and and more new relations from them.

You acquire a supply of ideas in three ways: 1. by receiving sense impressions; 2. by analyzing ideas already in your mind from previous sense impressions (this analysis will break them up into simpler ideas in an indefinitely continuing series); 3. by forming judgments about the ideas you have, you fashion new ones from them. For example: 1. If we perceive rainfall, we make the judgment, "It is raining," and we have an idea gathered from sense impressions. 2. If we further ask ourselves, "What is rain?" we think spontaneously of water, condensation, clouds, falling, puddles, and from this analysis we obtain more ideas about rain. 3. If, finally, we say to ourselves, "Suppose it rains too hard all at once?" we can come to a new idea, i.e., "flood," which is a synthesis of several ideas.

Reasoning is the third of the three R's. It is usually referred to as 'rithmetic, which is the simplest way of introducing the human mind to abstract thought. Arithmetic, however, is only a beginning, and, as education progresses, the third R grows into higher mathematics, science, philosophy, and theology. When a student reasons, he performs one of the two most human acts possible to him (the other being a deliberate act of the free will). We hardly need to stress, then, how important the reason is as an object of education. Any system calling itself educational which neglects this phase of human life would seem to be a living contradiction, and, therefore, devoid of meaning.

B. MEMORY

Memory is the foundation of all thinking. You cannot think without a supply of ideas, and you keep a supply of ideas by remembering. A memory, therefore, is an absolute necessity for a rational being. God has endowed all of us with memories, but He has left it to us to improve and perfect their functioning. The training of the memory will consist in developing, by means of mechanical and intellectual aids, the faculty He gave us until it is working at the peak of its efficiency.

The memory is the faculty by which we keep ideas before our minds, or, if they were acquired some time past, bring them back at will from that mysterious storehouse of the mind which no one, even today, understands. How we can apparently forget things and later recall them is a mystery. But this need not concern us at the present moment. Our objective, at this time, is to discuss the memory with the intention of profiting by what we know about it.

Not all men have the same kind of memory. Some can remember with greater ease things they have seen. Others are better at remembering what they have heard. Still others like to use the support of other senses when they are memorizing, for instance, repeating names aloud, or writing things down to fasten them in the mind. If you are wise, you will analyze yourself to see whether you have a memory which is predominantly based upon sound, or one which works best when aided by sight. If yours is the former, you should do your studying with the help of your hearing as much as you can. You should recite aloud to yourself, listen carefully in class, and, when going over your notes, try to remember how the instructor said it.

If you are the kind of person who remembers more easily what he has seen, you will try to reduce everything to writing, diagrams, pictures, outlines, statistical charts, and any other visual aids you can invent. Since sight memory is the commonest, visual aids are much in vogue in education today. We agree that their usefulness is great, and that they do not merely fasten things in the imaginative memory, but also teach with vividness, interest, and effect. Yet, like all good things, they are capable of being abused by imprudent use or over-use. Your memory is not only a sensitive faculty, but also a spiritual power. The spiritual memory, or the faculty which recalls abstractions, is not developed directly. It is improved by freeing it more and more from reliance on sense impressions and stimuli so that it is given a chance to work by itself. It is in pampering the sense of sight by burying the spiritual memory under an avalanche of sense impressions that visual aids are abused.

The memory you already have can be trained to do its work better, but you cannot acquire more of a memory than you have, nor can you trade it in for a different kind. Since the faculty is a natural gift, it is to be accepted and trained. There is no one who does not need memory training, but only the idiot wastes his time regretting that God did not give him a different kind of memory.

C. ANALYSIS

Analysis is the activity performed by human beings when they take something apart in order to discover its nature. At this moment we are only interested in intellectual analysis, which may be employed in the following ways: 1. by dividing a complex idea into simpler elements: for example, the concept "war" may be analyzed into "air war," "battle," "strategy," "desolation," and so on; 2. by tracing the history of an effect back to find the cause or causes which produced it: for example, that you have a cold may be the present sad state of affairs and an analysis of the last few days, recalling exactly what you did during that time, may show you how you caught it; 3. by searching for reasons to support a conclusion already in existence: for example, the conclusion may have been given you that intercollegiate athletics are harmful to education. The analysis would consist of an investigation into the effects of athletics on the college athletes, the student body, the curriculum, attendance at class, and other things capable of proving or disproving the conclusion.

Analysis, if we may be paradoxical, is constructive destruction. It is similar to digestion in the physical order. By analysis, the food of the mind is dissolved in order that osmosis (reflection, which we shall treat next) may take place, and thus develop an educated man.

Analysis, therefore, is a necessary adjunct of education. Unless you learn things according to their reasons and causes, you will not know them in a rational, human way. Without analysis, you will have recorded your learning in a superficial manner, as though you had written it on a piece of paper. If you have not been trained in analysis, you will not be able to synthesize reliably, because you will not have learned how things are made. Before you can produce something original, you must know the various methods of production from beginning to end. The wisdom of the ages must be at least partially in your possession before you can add your small contribution to it.

On the other hand, even though you may be skilled in analysis, you have no assurance, therefore, that you will be creative. We shall say more later about synthesis, but for the moment, let it stand that, although synthesis depends on analysis, it does not automatically follow from it.

All subjects may be treated analytically, but theology, philosophy, and the natural sciences are especially given to this process. Hence, these subjects can be used in education to very great advantage. If we may venture a cautious generalization, those subjects which lend themselves most readily to analysis and synthesis have the highest educational value, because they reach the student at his highest and deepest human level. For the same reason, we may say that any subject is capable of assisting toward an education inasmuch as it can be treated from the analytical-synthetic viewpoint.

D. REFLECTION

We now come to the last division of our discussion of thought, namely, reflection. This is the habit of pondering over things, slowly and carefully, musing about them, turning them over and over in the mind without haste or anxiety. Note that analysis is woven through reflection, but that the latter goes far beyond mere analysis. The reflective habit is rare today because of the twin demons, hurry and noise. Reflection must take place in peace and quiet, and it cannot be forced or hastened.

During World War II, there were given in colleges what they called "accelerated courses." By means of these, it was possible to complete the ordinary four-year college course within two years by going to class all year around and not taking any vacation. That this system was an emergency measure was its only excuse, for it allowed no time for reflection and was merely instructional, not educational. It permitted the brighter students to memorize a few things faster than they otherwise would have. The majority became mentally fagged and did not learn nearly as efficiently as they would have in the four-year course.

The real secret of learning lies in reflection, for by this means you are enabled to absorb what you have studied. That which you have learned is assimilated into your very being. But if you do not reflect, your learning remains on the surface and is easily rubbed off. Or else, if it does not entirely vanish, you use it without full realization of all its implications. The ordinary person needs time in order to perceive all the relations possible in a group of ideas. You cannot intuit everything at once. This time must be filled with reflection about what you have learned. In that way you grow into the matter, as it were; you develop with it, and it develops you. It becomes a living part of you, and you act upon it, sometimes without realizing it.

By means of reflection, there occurs a mysterious process called intuition—a seeing into an idea so that it is realized as never before. Intuition is sight. It is a firm grasp of something so that the knowledge is now unshakable. All men recognize the difference between knowing something, and then, one day, after long acquaintance with it, receiving a sudden burst of light: "Oh, now I see!" You have gained a sudden and clear vision of the subject which you never had before.

Intuition begets conviction. When you have seen something, no one can convince you that you haven't. If you see it snowing, no one, no matter what profound arguments he may use, can shake you in your conviction that it is snowing. If you are not too sure that you have seen it, the case may be otherwise. But if you really have seen, then arguments to the contrary mean nothing. Intuition happens the same way. If by reflection you have one day come to the sudden realization: "So, that's it!" no one is going to be able to convince you that "that isn't it!"

All men need convictions; the more they have, the more resolute men they become. Conviction is different from stubbornness. The latter is merely clinging to one's own preferences without sufficient reason. Conviction is certainty based on adequate and proven reasons. We may speculate that the reason why the modern generation is so worried, and has such difficulty coming to decisions, is that moderns do not take enough time for reflection, and thus do not build up enough convictions within themselves. They live speedily and superficially, and this most notably in the realm of the mind.

CHAPTER XVI

The Necessity of Religion

→»→»→»«←«←«←

To certain persons, it may seem to be a somewhat unusual idea to demand that a student be educated to religion, or *in* religion. The prevailing assumption expressed frequently in the everyday world is that religion is an entirely personal matter, something which exists between the individual and God alone. If this assumption were to be taken literally, no third party could say anything authoritative to you on the subject of religion, because if God has spoken to you, who else would have the right to tell you anything different?

The teaching of religion is based upon reality as we know it from sense experience, the use of reason, and revelation. It starts with the existence of God. Man not only can, but does recognize God's existence. The average man, when off guard, instinctively acts and thinks as though there were a God. He is impressed by the tremendousness of the universe into this tacit admission. Those with greater intellectual ability can argue metaphysically to the existence of a Supreme Being who is one, personal, and infinite. A further step in reasoning shows that God is the Creator of all things.

And here the practice of religion becomes a necessity. The Creator-creature relationship demands a certain way of life in the creature as its immediate consequence.

Since God is the Creator, all things are completely subordinate to Him. Not only the stars and the planets, the seas and the things that live in them, all plant and animal life, but man also must live according to the will of God. Upon man, as the lord of creation, falls the obligation of searching for and finding the will of the Creator in his regard, and then, doing it.

To help toward this goal, revelation was given to man a long time ago because, without it, he could not reach his final supernatural end. But once that revelation was given, it had to be transmitted from generation to generation by the men to whom it had been entrusted. Some of it was put in writing which we call the Scriptures, but the main point was that a body of men entrusted with the revelation was required to pass it down to the end of time.

This "handing down," or tradition, was to be done according to the ordinary methods in use among men. They were not to expect the continuance of supernatural revelation. That would be to look for continued miracles as the ordinary thing, and man has no right to expect that from God. On the contrary, man is left to himself to expand, develop, and apply revelation to the many circumstances of life. This we call theology and religion.

In addition to revelation as a source of the knowledge of God, man also has his senses and reason. By the aid of these, he can penetrate extensively into the existence of God and the nature of His Being. The creature can learn of the Creator's infinite perfections—His mercy, justice, goodness, love, and so on. He can read the history of God's dealings with man. He discovers from the use of his senses and intelligence that God actually has given a revelation to man, and further, what the details of that revelation are—the Incarnation, the Redemption, the institution of the Church, and God's commission to it to be His representative among men, and how that Church is to teach mankind authoritatively the revelation first given by God.

The need for education in religion becomes more acute the further we delve into the content of revelation. The student finds that God has not only told men about Himself, but that He has also indicated how He, God, wishes them to worship Him. Men come to know of the Great Sacrifice of the New Law through revelation. They hear of the sacraments, particularly of the Eucharist. They discover that God demands prayer from them, both as individuals and as a Church. It becomes clear, therefore, that the practice of religious rites is demanded by God, and that the only way those rites can be fully known and exercised is by education in religion. It stands to reason that man is not allowed to make up his own kind of religious rite. That would be possible only on the assumption that God had not revealed His will in the matter.

Even more intricate than the practice of proper religious worship is the exact fulfillment of the moral law in all its minute details. God's dominion covers every single moment of the life of every man. If it did not, God would cease to be God—He would cease to have the absolute and complete control over man that His nature as Creator demands.

In the life of every man there are countless successions of activities, many of which are deliberate. These deliberate acts have moral value: 1. because the act itself is either good or bad; 2. because it is done for a purpose which is either good or bad; 3. because it is done in circumstances which make it either good or bad. All of a man's deliberate acts, therefore, are worthy of praise or blame before God. In order for him to increase the number of the praiseworthy and to decrease the number of the blameworthy acts, a man needs to be taught, owing to the great variety and complexity of the acts possible. Because of the effects of original sin a man standing alone has too much against him. In addition to help from God, he also needs instruction in how to overcome the results of original sin, and encouragement to fight against them.

There is a difference between the fulfillment of the law in its essentials and in its perfection. Man must observe the essentials of the law in order to be saved. God has demanded that His creatures keep a certain number of precepts under pain of eternal punishment. This necessity grows out of the infinite perfection of God's nature. Since He is what He is, things could not be otherwise. However, he who loves God will strive with might and main to keep even the smallest details of the law with minute perfection. This will not be due to exaggerated legalism, but to the desire of one who loves to please Him whom he loves.

Thus, briefly, we see the reason for religion in education, or the training of man in the domain of religion. The existence of God and the consequent relationship between God and man demand that human beings be trained and developed in that relation. It is not a situation which will develop of itself. Witness the men of today! If you were to be taught everything else under the sun except religion, you would develop into a one-sided creature. The "one thing necessary" would be lacking. You would be good for everything, perhaps, except for that which is most fitting to your dignity as a creature of God. In this you would be wanting, and the absence would destroy all the good you might otherwise do in the fields wherein you have been trained.

Religion is not a subject to be taught, but an area of education. If you wish to sum up the objectives, or the meaning, of that area, you might say it is union with God. Beginning with apologetics, and working through the various treatises of dogma, moral theology, canon law, Church history, asceticism, and mysticism, you will discover that all of them have as their ultimate goal the ever closer union of a man with God. Hence, the layman is as much obliged to study them, for his personal profit, as the priest. The difference will lie in the way they are studied. The priest must study them more technically because he is to use them later as tools for the sake of others. The layman has every right, and also the duty, to know as much theology, and to use it for his own benefit, as the priest.

CHAPTER XVII

Aesthetic Development

➤➤-➤➤-➤➤«««-«««-«««

Aesthetics, in its most general signification, is the subject of good taste. While it is true that aesthetics is more commonly understood to refer to the perception of the beautiful, that usage would seem to limit its meaning too much. Not every use of the aesthetic faculty is concerned directly with what you would call the beautiful. If that were true, you might conclude that the aesthetic faculty lies dormant most of the time in most people, and is non-existent in many others. That it may lie dormant in many persons let us admit for the sake of argument, but that it does not exist in many, we deny.

Good taste varies markedly from person to person. Some never exhibit an appreciation of beauty as it is understood by the accepted canons of criticism. As a matter of fact, these persons may not even show vestiges of common, ordinary good taste. But if you observe closely, you will see that they have what we may call a "rebellion point," beyond which they will be shocked, offended, and their aesthetic feelings hurt. They really do not lack an aesthetic faculty; theirs is simply unusual or untrained. All men have within themselves those moments of recognition, appreciation, awe, and a kind of breathlessness at something they describe as beautiful. The nature of the object will range from a Sistine Madonna to a formula in astrophysics, but the reaction will be genuinely aesthetic.

Education, or educators (and by that we mean students, faculty, administration, parents, state, *et al.*), must recognize that this sense of beauty, fitness, good taste, or whatever they may wish to call it, exists in all men. It should be an object, therefore, of education in all men, even though there may be need for digging, in many students, to discover it. And, as students, you should consciously work upon your own aesthetic faculty throughout your college life, even though your college may have no specific courses or means of developing it. It lies so close to the center of a man's being that in many there is something akin to a feeling of shame at exposing it. They act as though they were turning themselves inside out whenever they express in any way their reaction to beauty. In addition to this natural repugnance, there is the added difficulty that, since taste is such a personal thing, and since it varies so much, you may hesitate to expose yourself to the contradictions, arguments, and even ridicule which the ignorant are always quick to employ in this matter.

Some men can be roused to ecstasy by a painting; others need the impact of a symphony. One man will be held in awe by the contemplation of a suspension bridge; another will not even notice the bridge as he rides across it in a bus, reading a book of poetry. There are those who can sit for hours drinking in the grandeur of a range of mountains; others would become impatient if they were deprived of the smelly cacophony of the city. You cannot predict how any person will react aesthetically, because the mood he is in will influence his reaction.

The first purpose of the aesthetic faculty is to enable you to sense the sublimity and beauty of God through His creation. It is also a gift given to help you endure what you cannot avoid, and to provide you with a blessed means of escape from the drabness of life.

The ordinary, everyday use of the aesthetic faculty does not involve anything worth dignifying by the name of beauty. It is taken up with such commonplace matters as neatness, cleanness, order, and so on, which are, as it were, channels leading into the sea of beauty. They partake somewhat of the sea they feed, but they are at best pale imitations of its awesome reality. You should not despise them because they are so little, usual, or insignificant. They have their uses, for it is of them that the good life is made. An appreciation of them will make your student life more pleasant and will permit you, in turn, to make life more bearable for others. Inasmuch as you esteem neatness, you will probably be proportionately neat. If you are neat, you will be that much easier on others. The same may be said for the other commonplace manifestations of the aesthetic faculty.

The one dynamic manifestation of the aesthetic faculty, namely, the creative or productive urge, we shall call the power of synthesis.

SYNTHESIS

To begin with, it must be admitted that synthesis could be considered as a part of expression. Yet, it seems preferable to include it under aesthetics, in view of the fact that a man rarely creates, produces, or makes something without, at the same time, trying to make it as beautiful as he can. Men who are forced by economic circumstances to make things by machine, or who work blindly on the production line, not seeing the final product of their efforts, and, hence, who are not striving for beauty in their work, are not acting in a human way. They have become parts of the machines they use. Man has a creative urge to make things from the beginning to the end himself, and to make them well. You can see this tendency manifested in the way men try to ornament buildings, parks, cars, and so on. They strive not only to make things be, but also to make them beautiful.

We say, then, that all men are endowed with the power of synthesis. This possession is part of the human heritage of being made to the image and likeness of God, the Creator. But not all of you will have this faculty in the same degree. In some, it will appear in a very rudimentary way; in others, it will bear the mark of genius. But all of you possess it, at least in the ability to daydream, wherein there seems to be nothing but the first faint urge to create. The genius makes his daydreams come true; education can assist the ordinary man toward the same end.

Since all men have the foundational urge to create, you should develop this in yourself as far as you are capable. You should stimulate first the desire to accomplish things. If possible, you should obtain the encouragement and help of your teachers, but if that cannot be had, go ahead on your own. Plan to accomplish something outstanding during your life. What it may be is not as important as the fact that it will be your own. It may be something made with hands, such as the actual building of a house, garage, furniture, a book, a play, or a painting. If you have the ambition to use to the utmost the creative faculty within you, you will approach your schooling in an entirely different spirit. Your studies may quite possibly take on more the quality of an adventure, leading to unknown conquests, with undreamed of possibilities stretching out ahead.

Too often this creative faculty is smothered under tons of economic "necessities." Making a living, paying the bills, keeping your job are important, but they need not take up all the time of an educated man. Some of the effects of your education should teach you how to budget not only your money, but your time also, so that you will always have sufficient leisure to apply to those things which are more in keeping with human nature.

In addition to the desire to create, there is another aspect to the synthetic process, namely, the ability to plan. This is a not inconsiderable gift in a human being. It assists you to look into the future, to foresee difficulties, to anticipate the actions of others, and to remain just a step ahead of the present. Some call it foresight, but there is nothing mysterious about it. Its development calls for as much study as possible of the present and the past, for it is from these that the future arises. Since the future can never be completely divorced from the past, those who despise the past are destroying the future. It is not that you are to learn to live in the past, but rather to collect from it that which is good so that you may, in the future, create that which is better.

It follows almost as a necessary conclusion from what has been said, that history and literature are the important subjects in the development of the synthetic power. These two subjects present the achievements of the past and the present—the one factually, the other inspirationally. In them we meet the great men of the past and present, in their actions and in their aspirations. From history and literature should come the force of example and inspiration sufficient to arouse all but the most sluggish temperament. If you know your history, you know the possibilities of the future; if you know your literature, you will want to actualize those possibilities.

Another step of the greatest importance in the process of synthesis is persistence. The creative world is littered with the wrecks of those who had desires, perhaps laid grandiose plans, and never finished. Production of any sort is hard, laborious, frustrating. It is possible that you have forgotten what is written in the book of Genesis: ". . . cursed is the earth in thy work; with labor and toil shalt thou eat thereof all the days of thy life. Thorns and thistles shall it bring forth to thee; and thou shalt eat of the herbs of the earth. In the sweat of thy face shalt thou eat bread till thou return to the earth, out of which thou wast taken: for dust thou art, and into dust thou shalt return" (Gen. 3:17-19). This is the curse put by God upon man because of original sin. Anyone who hopes to escape from it is fatuous. Even the bare effort to remain alive is burdened by it, and the more so will be the effort to accomplish greatness.

You must not expect to succeed at anything without correspondingly great toil. If you are convinced of this, much of the sting will be taken from your inevitable failures, for failures there must be. This conviction will also brace you for the strong and persevering effort needed to rise above mediocrity. The reason there are so few great men in the world is that it takes so much toil, self-denial and real suffering to become great. It is not because only a few have the talent or the intelligence. God is not so stingy with His gifts. There are many "mute inglorious Miltons" in the world simply because they do not have Milton's courage and determination to do something great.

Without synthesis, analysis is sterile. Analysis dissects the subject and aids in its assimilation.

When you have analyzed something, you have a good idea of how it is made; you could then hand it back, if required, exactly as you received it since you have taken it apart and put it together again. In order that there be original production, it is further required that you submit it to lengthy reflection until it has become part of you. After sufficient pondering, you will begin to reassemble that which you have analyzed, but the reassembling will now include more than the thing itself. Reflection will have so united you with your subject that, when you begin to rebuild it, you will unconsciously inject a part of yourself into it. In such wise does synthesis become an original product. You are expressing yourself as well as your subject, and you will do it differently from anyone else's way of expressing the same subject—always provided there has been a period of solid reflection upon it.

The product which you have created need not be something particularly striking. It certainly does not have to be a work of genius. It will merely be your own. It will have the stamp of your personality on it and, in that much will be inimitable. Perhaps, after long years of effort, perhaps much sooner, you will begin creating more strikingly original products. That remains to be seen.

The worth of this ordinary creativity need hardly be argued. God has made no two men alike, and the least they can do to honor and thank Him is to preserve their own uniqueness in whatever they do, instead of permitting their individuality to be drowned under a spate of conventional re-actions. The world will be a better place for their having been in it if they thus cooperate with God's gifts.

Education of the synthetic faculty will produce creative writers. Many a student who would never otherwise have thought of it will be lured into that field by being educated creatively. In addition to writers, this attention to synthesis will also beget productive scientists, artists, businessmen, and so on. Yet, not everyone will become eminent. That is too much to expect. Among the general run of students, the thing to hope for is that they will become original thinkers who will not be led by cant phrases and catchwords. When they speak, they will not mouth that which they last heard, but will utter thoughts of their own, originated under the stimulus of reflection and synthesis. Finally, our educational system will produce sympathetic administrators who will have been themselves trained to think creatively. They will be interested in stimulating their subordinates to productivity because they will understand what the desire to create is and they will offer all the help they can toward it.

CHAPTER XVIII

The Significance of Discipline

>>>->>>->>>-<<<-<<<-<<<

Discipline is the imposition of control from the outside when the person's self-control is either weak or untrained. Its aim, therefore, is to teach you to control yourself. The more self-control you have, the less you notice the restraint of discipline, unless the latter has degenerated into petty tyranny, because discipline is never an end in itself in education. It is intended, primarily, as a strong adjunct to the training of the will, and, secondarily, as a protection for public order.

The need for discipline arises out of the effects of original sin. Had there been no original sin, there would be no internal disorder in men, and, therefore, no external disorder in the world. As it is, all human beings must have, at least in the beginning of their lives, and many of them for their entire lives, the restraining force of discipline. They must learn to keep a fundamental order which is based upon the law of God. Some of you students learn this lesson early in your lives, and, for you, discipline never offers any problems.

Others, either through a perversity of nature, or because of some inherent mental incapacity, learn more slowly or even not at all. They are education's problem children—objects of pity, but never of trust.

The order in the world, from your viewpoint as an individual student, may be divided into three parts: 1. the order within yourself; 2. the order existing between you and the rest of mankind; 3. the order which you must keep among other persons. All the order in the world resolves itself into these three divisions; and if you are well educated in them during your school days, you will be able to take care of yourself as a Christian gentleman and an educated man for the rest of your life.

The three may be designated by a number of different names. For the sake of convenience we shall call them: 1. self-control, 2. reciprocal-control, 3. external-control. If anyone wishes to call them by other names, he is at full liberty to do so.

A. SELF-CONTROL

Self-control, a character trait infrequently stressed today, consists in the ability of the will to guide the person so that all choices made and actions performed will be in accordance with right reason and the law of God. It is possible, without self-control, to go through your entire life led by things rather than by reason or revelation. If you are not in command of yourself, caprice, passion, temperament, bodily indisposition, or other men will take over and rule you—usually to your own destruction. The importance of training in self-control in education needs no further argument.

The strength gotten from command over yourself enables you to use discrimination in employing the talents you have developed. You may know from reason that you should not read this particular book. Knowing it from reason will not be enough; you must have the strength of will not to read it. Or, this other book which is dull and lengthy may have been assigned for extra reading. Only a man who has a controlled character will make himself read it. Again, you may have the entire theory of salesmanship so that you can pass the strictest examination in it. But unless your character has been developed, you will not be able to use this theory under the adverse conditions you will often meet. You will more often permit your prejudices, or your temper, or some other uncontrolled factor to interfere and ruin the sale.

There is an old saying to the effect that "you cannot control others unless you first control yourself." The reason is simple. If a man does not have control over himself, he is unstable, unpredictable; he does not understand the difficulties of others, and he ends up in internal chaos from which no order can come. Others, sensing his internal conflict, will lose their respect for him, and will pay no attention to his advice or commands. In order to bring an education to bear upon life, self-control is a first requisite.

B. RECIPROCAL-CONTROL

This consists in the management of yourself in your dealings with others. It is based upon the virtue of charity, although charity has a much wider extension and application. It is called reciprocal because all, without exception, are obliged to act in this controlled way toward one another. There are no privileged characters. All men have rights upon which others may not infringe, and, in the same way, all men have duties toward others, the fulfillment of which the others may legitimately demand. The result of this area of discipline will be a sense of social responsibility.

To become more concrete: suppose that you have been unjustly treated. Your ungoverned reaction will be an attempt to "get even." If you have a sense of social responsibility, you will at once realize that "getting even" never blots out the first wrong, but rather spreads and intensifies the evil. The good of society is harmed more and more, the more individualistically such things are handled. The lack of discipline in another never gives you an excuse for being undisciplined.

Let us take the problem from another angle. It may be that one student will be more gifted than, let us say, his roommate. Now, the one could go sailing along in his academic career, piling success upon success, with never a thought to the struggles and frustrations of the less gifted man. The world will applaud his success and think nothing more about it. On the other hand, because of a sense of social responsibility, the bright student may reason that it would be better for the whole of society if he spent some of his genius in helping another less favored student. If he does this, he may not attain to such great success, although he will undoubtedly go far; but society as a whole will be better, in that education will have been spread farther than it would if he had kept to himself. This is a small illustration of a God-like quality. For as the goodness of God is spread abroad throughout His creation because God loves us all, so the creature imitates his Creator by spreading abroad goodness, even at some expense to himself. But it takes a disciplined man to do it.

One final concrete instance: it may never occur to you that being restricted in time and place in the use of tobacco has anything educational about it. Yet if you will attempt to understand why such orders are given, and if you will strive to carry them out to the best of your ability, you will be training yourself in self-restraint for the benefit of others. You will be developing a sense of social responsibility; you will be educating yourself.

C. EXTERNAL-CONTROL

The third objective of discipline is to train the individual to control others. It is part of the duty of an educated man to keep order among those whom he has in charge, that he may guide them for their own good and for the good of society. We say it is the duty of an educated man to keep order in others; he is not permitted to shirk it.

To keep order in others is not a pleasant job. No one likes to be a disciplinarian. It is a thankless task, yet a necessary one. Just as the educated man had to be trained in discipline in order that he might be fully educated, so he must train others for the same purpose, when it comes his turn to be an educator. Every adult has the duty to be at least an informal educator—especially of his children—and those who have charge of others must train them in discipline.

God has so arranged things that His government of the world is to be carried on through human representatives. Every man, therefore, who wields legitimate authority acts in the place of God. This demands a reciprocal obligation. The one who commands must never exceed his authority, nor must he abuse it. The one who obeys must see God in his superior, and must respect the authority of God in all that is lawfully commanded.

The obligations of those in authority are very burdensome; they are a great strain and they take much time. Yet no one is permitted to avoid these obligations once he is in a position of responsibility. It is sinfully selfish to accept the pleasures of power without its burdens. Education in discipline will train the student to accept his share in the government of the world, no matter how small or how large it may be.

D. ATHLETICS

At once, we must state that we are discussing athletics here solely from the disciplinary standpoint, and, furthermore, that by athletics we mean not only competitive sports, but all forms of exercise fit to develop the physique. We place athletics under the general heading of discipline because proficiency in them requires self-control. A man cannot even walk in a straight line unless he has control over his body. The more complex the form of athletics, the more control over the body is needed in order that it may obey the commands of the mind in performing the various gyrations required by the sport.

Athletics will develop you in the three ways already described. We may finish off what we have been saying about self-control by remarking that no one can even cut a respectable figure in the use of dumb-bells, much less with a tennis racket, or on ice skates, unless he has, by patient training, disciplined the muscles required for each specific exercise. If for no other reason than this, athletics would be worthwhile.

Every student should, if physically capable, have some experience in athletic training, in order that he may be able to use the material part of his nature for the glory of God and the salvation of his soul.

As for reciprocal-control and external-control, any one who has tried to become skilled athletically knows from personal experience how difficult they are. This knowledge causes to arise within him a feeling of respect for those who have tried and succeeded. He learns in contests to take into account the worth and ability of an opponent so that he not only strives to win, but also guards against defeat. He learns, by defeat, to be a generous loser, as well as, by victory, to be a gracious winner. Through the experience of both, he is better equipped to approach the ups and downs of life with less pride and bitterness, and with more humility and detachment.

The experienced athlete has had the opportunity to learn that leadership means inspiring by excellence, not coercing through fear. He has seen others follow because they were led; he has found that they obeyed because they respected, and imitated because they admired. Athletics have a place in education. They not only give the excess energy of youth a morally good outlet, but they also, when handled aright, have a strong influence in building character. A complete education must include athletics.

PART III

The Technique

❯❯❯❯❯❯❯❯❮❮❮❮❮❮❮❮

CHAPTER XIX
Definite Goals

>>>->>>->>><<<-<<<-<<<

1. When you set yourself to study, you should have two distinct purposes in mind: first, the remote aim of your future career; and second, the more proximate end of your mastery over this particular subject. Since your entire college course should be inspired by these two purposes, they should be as precise and clear as you can make them. It is never wasteful to spend time pondering your vocation, your career, and your plan of action in college. In the end, it will pay you to put some time on these thoughts at regular intervals, in order to continue the stimulation of your efforts. Hence, let us begin this section of the discussion on how to study by considering the usefulness of definite goals.

2. The first result of having a well defined aim in view when you study will be an increase of interest, because of the certainty of where you are going. Uncertainty is annoying, at best, and it is human to desire the security of a definite direction for your efforts. Perhaps much of the drudgery of your past study has been due to not understanding

the purpose of the whole course. You may have been plodding along from day to day with no particular end in view, merely memorizing successive fragments of matter which had no apparent bearing upon each other. You must make it your practice to find out for yourself exactly where each single course is leading, and as much as you can, find the means of getting there.

3. Once you know where you are going, you should scan each section of the material to see whether or not you are following in the direction it is leading, and, if so, by what route it proposes to get there. The view of the end should be an incentive to get started, an attitude which will help you to put forth worthwhile effort.

4. You should also look for collateral material which will contribute toward your subject's goal. Let us suppose you are studying, under the heading of economics, the structure of a corporation. Then, as collateral matter, you could consult *The Wall Street Journal* in order to follow the daily activities of a certain corporation. You would note the value of its stock on the exchange; you would watch the financing of the corporation through new bond issues, the redemption of old bond issues, and the issuance of new stock; you would discover the changes in personnel of the corporation; you would keep abreast of the research and development of its products; and you would be informed of the latest Congressional legislation af-

fecting the corporation. The use of this sort of material during your study will associate classroom theory with actual living practice, thus aiding your memory and helping you to become an expert. The same thing might be done with the study of language. As collateral matter, the country whose language you are studying should become an object of your close and constant scrutiny. By following the fortunes of the country, you would not only learn the language, but also become an expert in the affairs of that country.

5. Since your study is a steady progress toward a definite end, signposts along the way are most important helps to a safe journey. The use of maps, charts, pictures, news articles, radio broadcasts, television, advertisements, and many other similar things will be an important guide along the way. They appeal to all your senses, and you thus learn through many different channels at once.

6. Gradually the more familiar you become with the various subjects of the curriculum, the more you tend to see your daily life "through their eyes," as it were. Your history becomes a springboard from which you can plunge into a better understanding of modern history. Your English courses train you to read with discernment, and to attend the theatre with greater appreciation of the technical structure of plays.

7. Insensibly your interests will become wider.

You will learn by experience the many connections existing between the various subjects of the curriculum. This is usually a revelation to beginners. They are so used to compartmentalizing their knowledge and their activities that it never occurs to them that God intended all life to have a unity, with Him as its center.

8. Another advantage from linking life to study will be that the dead print of the textbook will begin to come alive in your own life. The realization will grow on you that textbooks do not just "occur," but that they are written by men who generally know what they are talking about, and each of whom has a purpose in writing his particular book. Further, the reason why this particular textbook was chosen by the instructor was because he thought it served its purpose best of any that he knew.

9. Not everything said by the professor in class needs to be kept in your notes, nor is everything in the textbook to be memorized. In order to grasp the essence of any course, it is necessary to be able to see which are the more, and which the less, important details. Doing this will minimize your burden by helping your memory, but it will demand knowledge of exactly where every part of the course leads. You must understand the end if you will properly evaluate the means.

CHAPTER XX

General Methods

~~»»-»»-»»«««-«««~~

1. Study will never become perfectly easy. It will always be necessary to spend disciplined effort in the pursuit of knowledge and, hence, a life habit of mortification will be a tremendous help to study. Lest you misunderstand, by mortification we mean the practice of self-denial, or doing things you do not like. For example, to deny yourself a cigarette when you feel like smoking, or to accustom yourself to sit up straight when you would prefer to lounge, will train you in the self-control necessary to keep you at your desk studying when you would much rather be out on the ball field. We may seem to be discussing a subject remote from the matter of study, but, remember, it is the same fellow who studies or lounges. Sitting at a desk does not change your nature; it merely changes your occupation.

2. Once you have decided upon a course of action, do not stop until you are finished. Naturally, this presupposes that you will think out your plans prudently before you undertake them. It is good to form the habit of following things through to a conclusion. If you do not learn to do this, you will

most likely fall into the opposite extreme, that is, of flitting from one project to another as soon as your initial interest lags. Since you may not find much of the enthusiasm of novelty in a collegiate course of studies, the practice of perseverance will habituate you to do things over extended periods long after the first impulse has worn off.

3. When you begin to study a subject, do not be in too much of a hurry to finish your chore. Never mind the speed at the start; that will come later. At first be interested in accuracy above all things. This will not easily be had when a new vocabulary or strange thought processes are mystifying you. Yet, every subject will have its own way of "getting there," and you should pay each the courtesy of becoming acquainted before you try to rush it off its feet. If a subject is worth study, it is worth careful study; and any subject in the college curriculum is worth study. Therefore, take your time at the outset; the speed will take care of itself.

4. We come now to a matter which can be expressed abstractly, and in principle, but which is difficult to explain in the concrete. We may state it thus: be sure external conditions favor a study atmosphere. By this we mean that there should be no distracting things—sounds, persons, or even odors (cooking, for example) present in the ideal place for study. Now just what constitutes a distracting thing will vary from student to student. For some of you, a radio going full blast offers no

distraction (so you say!), but others would be driven to flunking if they had to put up with it. Again, a loudly ticking clock will drive some students mad, while others will be merely stimulated by it to greater efforts. Each has to learn by experience what conduces to study in his own case, and what does not. The sincere student will observe his personal reactions, and will proceed accordingly.

5. A habit which is important but which takes self-denial to achieve is the habit of study immediately after class. Your normal tendency, at the end of a class day, will be to toss aside your books and hurry off to play and relax, or, perhaps, to work. You may justly argue that you are tired of study at the end of a class day, and do not work at the peak of efficiency when studying at that time. But the study we advocate here is not the exhaustive work usually meant by this word. We advise you to go over your lecture as soon as possible after it is finished in order to recall the important points made by the instructor. It need not take long. Yet, it will fasten the ideas in your mind so that your later study will be much more profitable both in memory and in understanding.

6. When you sit down at your desk to study, study at once! It is a common experience to be beset by subterfuges enticing you away from the work to be done. You will find yourself catering to a suddenly developed passion for neatness, as you industriously clean your desk and rearrange your

furniture. You will find that, up till now, you had forgotten to do some odd job which, of course, must be done at once. You may even become conscience stricken at the thought of certain letters which you should have, but have not, answered. You will want to do everything but study. If you will keep a close check on your actions, you will find yourself falling into this practice constantly. It is a trick of human nature to dodge the present, distasteful duty. Remember the danger, and you will be less prone to fall into it.

7. Have a study schedule and stick to it! It is too easy to be haphazard about what to study and when. Your daily life with its complexity may seem to argue against such a regimen, but if that objection prevails, it is a sign that instead of you controlling things, things are controlling you. With a little good will and planning, it is possible to draw up a respectable schedule wherein you will duly care for each subject over the course of a week. This will necessitate figuring out a time budget, but any sensible person who wishes to accomplish more than the essentials will have to budget his time. You will come to it sooner or later, and you may as well learn while you are young and adaptable.

8. One of the most efficient ways of studying is to use a pencil to make outlines. You should keep the pencil busy diagramming paragraphs, underlining words and sentences (don't do too much of

this or it will become meaningless), writing comments in the margins, jotting down questions to be answered later. Concentration will profit greatly from this practice, as also will your understanding and remembering of the subject matter. Needless to say, you should not write in books that are not your own, but in your own textbooks you may do as you please.

9. Review your subjects frequently. How frequently will depend upon the number of class periods per week, on the complexity of the subject, and on your ease in understanding it. It is clear that you will not be able to grasp all subjects with equal ease. Frequent reviews will make clear which subjects need more attention. There is no sense in dawdling over a subject which you have learned satisfactorily, when you might be spending the time more profitably on some others in which you are weaker. Your common sense will dictate that you keep asking yourself, "Do I really understand what this subject is all about?" If you do not, you will stop at once and not proceed beyond that point until you have conquered the difficulty. He is wasting his time who studies week after week without knowing what he is studying.

10. It helps toward learning if you can speak the matter aloud—either to yourself (if that is the best you can do!), or preferably to someone else. A sign of knowledge is an ability to communicate your subject to another. Unless you are able to put what

you know into words, you may well suspect your knowledge. Discussion with others gives them a chance to tell you whether or not you are making sense. When you recite to yourself or to others, the sound of your own voice may lead you to a better understanding of your topic.

11. Pause occasionally to analyze yourself, your methods, your achievements. An unbiased look at yourself will reveal your personal shortcomings as well as your abilities, for the average man will have both, and the educated man should be honest enough to admit both. A glance at your methods of study will go far toward showing their practicability, adequacy, or insufficiency. You may find that you can transfer a method from one subject to another with subsequent increase in efficiency. And finally, you should inspect your present achievements, such as grades, test results, and grasp of subject matter, as evidence of the application of your abilities and methods to given tasks.

12. Since bursting into the realm of study from something non-academic is a violent change and is hard on the will power, common sense dictates that you build a bridge for crossing from non-study to study. Therefore, when you sit down to study, use a warm-up drill first. This consists in doing something which is easy and familiar, yet which has the atmosphere of study about it. For example, a brief review of something you already know fairly well often gives the impetus and confidence to proceed

into difficult matter. Sometimes that running start over matter which should be familiar will show that it is not as familiar as you thought. Because most subjects in the curriculum move progressively from the less known to the better known, you will not properly understand what follows without a thorough understanding of what preceded.

13.   If you would be a good student, avoid too frequent social functions. It is not that you must become a recluse. You can still keep in touch with all that is going on in your social set, without being the first at every party or dance, and the last to leave. Virtue lies in the middle, and the middle course here is to appear occasionally, e.g., at the best events, and, for the rest, to remember that you are a student most of the time. If you attempt to attend everything, you waste much time, lose the recreational value, tire yourself for study, and retain memories which may distract you during study hours. You cannot concentrate on study, and on other things at the same time.

14.   When you have a problem in any field, approach it with method. A careful analysis should make clear to you its general nature. Thereupon you should attempt to reduce it to its component parts. To do this, you should be able to define all the pertinent terms, not only for the sake of clarity, but also for a better use of the tools of thought. Make sure that the difficulty is really objective, that is, that it does not spring from your personal

prejudice toward the subject. You may expect to find factors in your problem which are not easy to handle. Some scholastic questions are capable of only one answer, such as those in mathematics; others can, perhaps, bear many coordinate solutions; still others may lead you no further than probable answers. Whatever direction the problem may lead, whichever way the facts may point, you should never hesitate to revise your theory to fit the facts. Unless you are sure of your facts, admit that your answers are tentative and that they await the test of further study or experiment. Always make a distinction between a theory and a proven conclusion. And finally, remember that the pursuit of truth demands the most unselfish honesty on the part of the searcher.

15. Do not attempt too many kinds of activity. Since your classroom studies are the most important, you should give priority to them. If you find that you can include some extra-curriculars without harming your class work, by all means do so. The outside activities are also educational, and every student should be able to carry at least one. However, give yourself a chance to study in the beginning, and take up the activities a little at a time.

16. Authorities say that you should study two hours for every one of class. If that sounds like too much, pause and think it over before tossing the advice aside. Study, as we have said, consists in

more than carelessly perusing the textbook. It means attempting to master the subject. If you find that you can master all your subjects in less than two hours of study for each hour of class, you are an unusual person.

17. Recognize early in your course that it is difficult to arrive at final answers about many things. Do not expect a ready and all-satisfying response from the instructor every time you ask a question. Since many pertinent questions require books to answer them adequately, you will be foolish if you fret at not receiving satisfaction "on the run" in the classroom. It is a sign of your advancement in wisdom when you have realized that clever answers are tremendously harder to find than clever questions.

18. Be slow to pass judgment on persons and things. Life is complex and the more you see, the more you will find that complete understanding of it is beyond you. Give the other fellow the benefit of the doubt always, and do not think that, because you can solve a problem which he cannot, you are, therefore, a better man than he. It may be that he has already solved, to his own satisfaction, many of your own private and most baffling problems. The tentative stand is the best on many issues. This does not mean that you must doubt everything that cannot be proved by experiment in a laboratory, but that you will only hold as certain those things which, one way or another, have

been proved to be certain. In the same way, do not deny the statement of an authority unless you have proof against it.

19. Work hard at the study of religion. You probably think you know the Catholic Faith fairly well since you may have had it in grade school and high school with good marks. But, remember that the study of religion in college will lead you more deeply into the subject than you ever went before, and that your Faith contains many mysteries which you must attempt to understand—as much as the human mind can. The study of religion is not the exclusive prerogative of priests. Since you laymen are also members of the Mystical Body, you must be intelligently apostolic, and to be apostolic you must know your Faith. You cannot know your Faith by studying it only when you have nothing else to do, or just enough to pass an examination.

CHAPTER XXI

Reading

※※※※※※※

1. Skipping words whose meaning you do not know is a practice which will prevent the development of your education. As you move through college taking up increasingly higher branches of study, you will be continually meeting new words, among them many that are highly technical. You should assist your maturing by making the closest possible acquaintance with as many of these words as you can, in order to increase your working vocabulary. As we have said, everyone has two kinds of vocabulary: the words which he recognizes when he reads, and the words he can call up at will when he writes or speaks. The former is always the larger, but the latter can be increased by the serious exercise of the former. For example, if you know what a certain word means when you meet it in a book, the more often you meet it in your reading, the more familiar you become with it, and the more likely you are to begin including it in your speech and writing.

2. When you read, be creative; that is, do not merely take in what you find on the printed page,

but let it stimulate your own thinking even as you read, so that you could almost write a page parallel to the one you are reading. The contents of this parallel page need not be too similar to the contents of the page you are reading. They may be concerned with anything that has been called up by the stimulation of the author's message. Yet, to be a creative reader you dare not rest with a bare survey of the printed pages. That will keep everything on the surface, and the real you underneath need not be stirred at all to respond to the meaning. To get the proper result, you must be alert enough to understand what you are reading, to be comparing it with many things you have read before, to be contrasting, arguing with the author, developing the subject along side lanes which will branch off from the main highroad. Even when you agree with what is written, do not allow the thought to rest but carry it on to further conclusions and applications fitted to your own life. You must, as it were, supply for the author's deficiencies, and appreciate it when he supplies for yours.

3. Never be satisfied with reading one book on a subject, for no one book can adequately cover any topic. One of the reasons is that each author will have written with a limited objective in view, unless he is compiling an encyclopedia. A second reason is that no one book, even an encyclopedia, is big enough to hold all that can be said, except about the most limited of areas. You might ask ten scholars to write a good sized book on the same

theme, and each work would be different from all the other nine, since each scholar would contribute something of his own to the subject. The art of reading, therefore, consists in going through a book at varying speeds. Where you find duplication of some other work, hurry on; where you find new matter or new treatment of old matter, pause, reflect, and permit it to become part of you.

4. Read beyond the subject at hand. Do not hesitate to follow some of the tangents, or to work out some of the by-products of your reading, for you will find much profit as well as interest in them. No subject stands completely alone. You cannot read in sociology without running into economics and psychology; a book on religion will touch upon metaphysics, history, ethics, and many other things. Going off on one or more of these side issues is never a loss of time, provided it does not take you from work that must be done. From tangents and by-products have come many discoveries and original ideas.

5. When you read, do so with a sense of having to give an account of the book to someone else. If you feel that you are going to have to describe, criticize, analyze, and evaluate this work before someone who will ask searching questions, you will be put on your mettle while reading, and the ideas of the book will be impressed upon your memory. You will thus find yourself reading more accurately and with greater attention to detail. Even

though you will not have to give a report, the practice will make you a careful reader, able to read between the lines and to see more than appears on the printed page.

6. If possible, make a preliminary survey of a chapter before beginning to read. First see it as a whole, and then go through it part by part. The familiarity thus gained will give more meaning to the chapter and the whole book. Analyze the contents and skip around here and there, reading passages at random. Dip into the index and look up a few items to see how they are treated. You are not reading in order to be kept in suspense. Remember, detective stories are the only books you read in order to be surprised.

7. When you have grasped the main idea of a paragraph, you can summarize it in a single sentence. Afterwards, you may connect these sentences together in outline form in order to catch the bearing of the entire chapter. If your understanding of the chapters is thus clear and comprehensive, you will be better able to decide whether or not to continue reading the book. You may find that your chapter analysis has shown you the uselessness of this particular book for further reading.

8. Before starting to read a book, do some independent thinking about its subject matter. As much as you can, recall your own knowledge of the topic and then read with the intention that

the book will augment your present store. For interest, predict to yourself what the author is going to say, and then read to discover if you have covered more territory than he, and to note how he differs from you in style, approach, and material. As your education advances, you may surprise yourself by your knowledge and ability.

9.   Do not skip such things as graphs, charts, maps, diagrams, tables, drawings, and other useful printed aids. They may be handy visual summaries of pages of text, or they may be pictorial guides through some rather abstruse passages to come. These aids more forcibly convey the meaning of statistics, principles, processes, geographical locations, and other useful knowledge. Things scattered over wide spaces or periods of time can be drawn together and summed up most easily in this way. When the author includes them in his work, he thinks that they are important. You should too!

10.   Sometimes it is very helpful to read by topics rather than to read any one book entirely. By this we mean that you should work through as many as ten books, not reading any of them completely, but only reading that which pertains to the subject you are studying. The purpose of this practice is to acquire a unity of understanding of the topic. You will see the ideas of many authors bearing on the same subject, at one time, and it will probably stimulate your own thinking more quickly than reading and following a single author would.

11.   Do not believe everything you read. The fact that something appears in print does not make it true. Read one author against another and try to substantiate their findings by your own experience or experiments. This is not to distrust everybody; it is simply using a prudent reserve in judgment. It is not scepticism, but caution, an antidote to the all too common human failing of believing the last thing read or heard. There is hardly need to point out that in the realm of religion, where authority is the strongest argument (the authority of the representative of God interpreting His revelation), this practice must be drastically curtailed. In religion, your own personal experience or any experiments on your part have nothing to do with the existence of revealed facts, or with the approved interpretation of the facts. For these matters your scepticism must be limited to testing the standing of the author, i.e., whether or not his work has the stamp of approval of the Church.

CHAPTER XXII

Use of the Library

‑⟫⟫‑⟫⟫‑⟫⟫⟨⟨‑⟨⟨‑⟨⟨‑

1. The decimal classification, originated by Melvil Dewey, and used in many libraries as the catalogue system, is based upon the following general divisions:

000	General Works
100	Philosophy
200	Religion
300	Social Sciences
400	Philology
500	Pure Science
600	Useful Arts
700	Fine Arts
800	Literature
900	History

A system of subdivision is then followed throughout these ten categories. If the subdivision is directly subordinate to the preceding category, it is numbered up the scale toward 999. For example:

000	General Works
060	General Societies
069	Museum Economy

069.1   Educational and Recreational Functions of Museums

069.13   Lending Objects from Museums

You will notice how *General Societies,* being a subdivision of *General Works,* keeps the "0" as its first number; the same thing is true of *Museum Economy,* and so for the rest. The reason *Lending Objects* . . . has a three (.13) rather than a one (.11) is that it is the third type of educational function mentioned. The first type would be ".11," the second type, ".12." Another example of the divisions of the Dewey System is:

100   Philosophy
110   Metaphysics
111   Ontology
111.1   Analysis of the Idea of Being
111.11   Existence

The same thing is true here. *Metaphysics* is the first subdivision of the category of philosophy; *Ontology* is the first subdivision of the category of *Metaphysics; Analysis of the Idea of Being* is the first subdivision of *Ontology*; and *Existence* is the first subdivision of the category *Analysis of the Idea of Being.* Note that *Ethics,* although a subdivision of philosophy, is not a subdivision of metaphysics. Therefore, ethics is classified under the 170 rather than under the 110 heading.

Let us consider one final series for clarity's sake:

700   Fine Arts
750   Painting
770   Photography

```
780       Music
782       Dramatic Music
782.1     Grand Opera
783       Church Music
783.2     Liturgical Music
783.25    Plain Song
```

Note how 782.1 is the first subdivision under *Dramatic Music,* how 783.2 is the second subdivision under *Church Music,* and 783.25 is the fifth subdivision under *Liturgical Music.* The Dewey System, as you can see, is very logical and quite easily followed.

2. The Library of Congress System, however, is based upon the alphabet. The main categories run as follows:

A   General Works—Polygraphy
B   Philosophy—Religion
C   History—Auxiliary Sciences
D   History and Topography—except America
E   America (General) and United States (General)
F   United States (Local) and America (except the United States)
G   Geography—Anthropology
H   Social Sciences—Economics—Sociology
J   Political Science
K   Law
L   Education
M   Music
N   Fine Arts
P   Language and Literature
Q   Science

R   Medicine
S   Agriculture—Plant and Animal Industry
T   Technology
U   Military Science
V   Naval Science
Z   Bibliography and Library Science

Each of the above main categories is subdivided according to letters of the alphabet. For example: B—Philosophy:

BC   Logic
BD   Metaphysics
BJ   Ethics

Subdivisions under these headings are identified by numbers. For example:

BD 10 — 41   Introductions to Philosophy
BD300 — 444   Ontology

If you learn the major categories as indicated by the letters of the alphabet, you will have no difficulty in locating the section of shelves containing the books you are interested in.

3.   If you wish to become proficient in the use of the library, you should familiarize yourself with the catalogue. Every library has a catalogue accessible to all, which may be consulted in order to save time in looking for books on the shelves, or for filling out request slips for books when the stacks are not open to the public. All the books in the library are catalogued under the name of the author, and under the title of the book. Usually,

they are also listed under subjects, and sometimes even under smaller divisions of the main subject. For example, a book on marriage may be listed not only under the heading of *Marriage,* but also under *Sacraments, Contraception, Divorce,* or other topics treated under marriage. In the upper left hand corner of the catalogue card are found the call numbers of the book, either Dewey Decimal System numbers or Library of Congress numbers, according to the system used by the library. If you are making out a request slip for the book, be sure to copy these numbers exactly as they are on the card, because they will lead the librarian directly to the book. If you are going to search for the book yourself, the call numbers, after a little practice, will be of equal help to you. If ever the book you want is in use, make out a request card for it, giving the title, author, call numbers, and your name and class, and leave this with the librarian. Your name will be put upon a waiting list and you will get the book as soon as it is available.

4. A certain portion of every week should be set aside for consulting the magazines which treat of the matter contained in your curriculum. For example, to mention only a few, in English, you should follow such books as *Vital Speeches* and *The English Journal;* in history, *The American Historical Review* and *Speculum;* in the social sciences, *The Journal of Political Economy, Foreign Affairs, The Quarterly Journal of Economics, The Social Service Review,* and *Psychological Ab-*

stracts; in education, *The Catholic Educational Review*; in philosophy, *The Modern Schoolman*; in religion, *The Catholic Mind* and *The Pope Speaks*. These are but a few of the many magazines which will be carried by college libraries. By going over them as they appear, you will soon discover your favorites, to which you can pay closer attention and thus keep abreast of your field. In addition to these, you should also keep in touch with periodicals of a more general nature which will inform you of the daily news, whether departmental—such as, education, religion, business, politics, international news—or general news. Some of the better known periodicals of this class would be *Time, Newsweek, U.S. News and World Report, The New York Times, The Wall Street Journal,* and a few other key publications. Let it become automatic with you to note the publisher, address, and subscription rates of these periodicals so that if you later wish to subscribe to one or more in your field, you will know where to write.

5. If you have to write a term paper or are copying some quotations from a book, or are merely making a reference for future use, it will save you much time to learn, once and for all, how to cite the source. First comes the author's name; next, the title of the book. Then comes the name of the city in which it was published, followed by the name of the publisher, and the date of publication. The last thing to be noted is the page of the reference. The copyright law protects the author

from plagiarism. One is not permitted to use copyrighted material as his own, nor to incorporate it into his writing, even though he gives proper credit to author and publisher. To use such matter, it is necessary to have the express permission of the copyright owners.

6. Acquaint yourself at an early date with the most important of the reference books in the library. Such books may be categorized as follows: the encyclopedias, Who's Who, almanacs, the book and periodical indexes, dictionaries, Roget's Thesaurus, collections of quotations, atlases, handbooks and yearbooks, United States Government publications, directories, catalogues, technical anthologies, compendiums, surveys, and so on.

7. Not all books are of equal value, nor will all be of equal use to you in your study. For example, some authors are of greater authority than others; some books are more scholarly than others. A selection will be necessary if you are not to waste time reading the less important, to the exclusion of the more important. Certain books will be ruled out of your reading lists because they belong on the Index of Forbidden Books; others will be forbidden by the natural law which demands that you remain out of the proximate occasion of serious sin. As for the rest, you must depend on good advice from authorities, or on your own skimming tactics before settling down to read the entire book. You must learn to evaluate individual books by

studying their tables of contents and indexes to see if they contain matter of interest and importance to you. Some knowledge of the author of the book you are about to read will help you to guard against possible prejudice or bias in his approach to his subject. One other thing to note is the date of publication. Since some fields are expanding and progressing at a tremendous rate, the year of publication may save you reading time by indicating that the book is out of date.

8. Bibliographies are lists of writings on certain circumscribed subjects. Some authorities condemn the making of bibliographies merely for the sake of making them. We might agree with this were it not for the fact that many students are completely ignorant of the books published in the field of their study. Hence, it would seem that if students could be induced to make up practice bibliographies on the subjects they are studying, it would have at least the effect of acquainting them with many books they might otherwise never hear of. For this reason, we recommend that once or twice during the course of your college career, you make a list of books on some subject that you have studied or will study. When making this list, be sure to do more than merely note the name of the author. Try to find out something about the book by skimming through it, tasting here and there. You may thus find yourself enticed into reading books that will do you a lot of good.

CHAPTER XXIII

Powers of Observation

->>>->>>->>><<<-<<<-<<<-

1. It is usually true to say that you will notice things in proportion to your interest in them. If you are indifferent to something, you will pay very little attention to it; but if you are vitally concerned, you will not miss anything connected with it. This is a clue to success in studies. Not all of us have an equal interest in everything we must study. Naturally, we prefer some subjects to others, and for various reasons. If you go through your college life studying only those things in which you find yourself engrossed, and give scant attention to the others, your total education will suffer. The problem for the student is to foster in himself an interest in all his studies. This can be done by remembering a few unnoticed things about human nature, which will therefore be true of you. a. The fact that you are not interested now, does not mean that you cannot become interested. b. Interest will be generated by trying to find something in the subject which has a direct bearing on your own life. c. One of the best ways to arouse interest is to realize that this study will be somehow profitable to you. d. A certain type of hostil-

ity engenders interest (We are all interested in our country's enemies!). e. Remember, interest need not indicate that you like a subject. f. You may some day wish you had been interested in this particular subject.

2. When you are in class, always pay close attention. Never daydream. You may think the professor is monotonous, or that the weather is oppressive, or that you do not feel so well today, or that the subject is useless. Chase these temptations away during the time of class and keep your mind on your work. We can tell you from personal experience that it is always possible to gain something worthwhile even from the dullest class period. What you gain from class will depend, in great part, on what you put into it. Your own attitude can make all the difference between an interesting and a boring class. Someone has said that there are no bores—only those who are bored. Act upon this assumption and you will profit much from class periods.

3. Always use your eyes and ears intelligently. Never just see something; see through it. Everything that exists has come into being through the use of an intelligence—either God's or some creature's. For example, dust on a window sill can be a clue to someone's personality; or scribbling on a blackboard, or a manner of dress, or a tone of voice, or the method of presentation of a lecture—all of these can be interesting points of observation

and will be a help to your learning and education. There is no more interesting subject for study than human beings. You can find vestiges of them everywhere, and traits which offer hints to their characters.

4. Occasionally it is fascinating to see things through the eyes of someone else. We are very personal in our approach to things; and if we do not make a deliberate attempt to be objective, we shall miss much. Try especially to see yourself as others see you. Listen to yourself recite sometimes and wonder what you would think of yourself if you were the teacher. Take some of the things you wrote when in high school and reexamine them. What do you honestly think of the fellow who turned in that stuff? Do you like him? Or do you think he is a mild fraud? Is there any room for improvement in him? You can grow up rapidly by adopting this attitude of objective self-criticism because you will cease to be childishly engrossed in yourself.

CHAPTER XXIV

The Reason

※»-»»-»»-«««-«««-«««

1. Learn early in your career not to be guided by your emotions. No matter how you feel about a difficulty today, you will probably feel different tomorrow. But, your knowing or thinking is an intellectual, spiritual act, and the chance of fickleness dominating the intellect is remote. The emotions are blind; even when they are heading for their proper objects, they tend to go in a blind rush. God gave them the intellect and will to guide and control them, lest they injure themselves, and consequently, cause harm to the whole person. One of your most important pursuits during your college years will be so to train your intellect and will that they will become competent guides for your emotions. The old advice about counting to ten when angry is solidly based; it gives you a chance to think before giving in to anger. Less easily perceived than anger is the emotional urge which tells you to cling to a conclusion you have formed—not because it is true, but because you like it. The subtle nature of this fault makes it a foe worthy of your respect. We all instinctively embrace certain ideas or habit patterns, which,

under the cold light of reason, will appear to be according to our taste, or aimed at our profit. That they are according to right reason is often an accidental circumstance.

2. You often hear it said that the truth hurts. Your complacent agreement with this dictum will suffer a rude shock when you do finally run into the truth, because the theoretical knowledge of the truth and the actual experience of it are not the same. Truth is hard and unyielding; it is no respecter of persons; it will not change to suit you. When you meet it, you may not recognize it: it will wear so hostile an appearance. But your education, if it is authentic, will teach you to face and accept the truth, no matter how unpalatable. The attitude of the educated man should be: "God is truth, and any part of the truth is a reflection of God. The truth, therefore, will be good for me in the total view of life, even though it may be temporarily uncomfortable." Hence, never run from the truth; confronting it will be best for you, for your neighbor, and for mankind.

3. It is difficult for beginners in life to distinguish between ideals and air-castles. Sometimes you will not be able to tell the difference between them without help from someone else. An ideal may usually be described as a lofty goal, not entirely beyond your ability, but not at all easily attained. An air-castle, on the other hand, is a lofty goal which, although extremely enchanting, is either

temporarily or permanently beyond your reach. Riding toward an air-castle on a white horse, clad in shining armor, is a thrilling occupation, but a total waste of time. To grit one's teeth and struggle toward an ideal is the work of a real man, especially in today's ideal-less world. What should you do about it in the practical order? If you are puzzled as to whether a certain project or way of life is an ideal or an air-castle, ask some older person whose judgment you respect. Usually another person can be objective enough to give you some sound advice which will save you much time and toil, or which will encourage you to keep plodding, no matter how hopeless it seems.

4. Do not be dazzled by the striking idea. Once a certain facility has been acquired through practice and experience, it is easy to be "brilliant," but it is not so easy to be profound. The emcees and wordy comedians of radio and television with their facile and flashy patter can give you a false sense of values. They can so influence your thinking that you will mistake the superficially brilliant expression for a deep thought. It would seem that how you say or write a thing is of much less importance than what you say or write. Some persons will never be witty; they are not endowed by God to be that way. But God has given all an intelligence which is capable of a profundity beyond our imagining. Develop your thinking; never mind the glitter.

5. Acquire the habit of classifying your information. Label it *certain, probable,* or *false.* You might also use the categories: *certain from experiment, certain from experience, certain from deduction,* or the like. In the category of *probable* you might note whether it is probable because of present information, or because of the impossibility of obtaining more information. These are not the only classes, but they are given to show how order may be kept in knowledge. This habit of classifying material will make your thinking very definite and clear by eliminating vagueness, inaccuracy, and other pests of scholarship.

6. Another way to strengthen your thinking is to devise your own examples illustrating the matter. It is easy to memorize the examples given in class or in the books, but it is not wise to do so. Study those which have been given in order to learn the exact point of the example; then, make up your own. This will prove that you have a proper grasp of the matter, that you really understand it and are not simply parroting what someone else has said.

7. It is always useful to work according to a logical plan. Do not be haphazard about anything, whether it is the order in which you study all your subjects, or the processes you use within the study of any one subject. If there is order, plan and logic in your work, you will remember it more easily,

you will know more about it, and you will present it more effectively. Although you should never study merely to obtain good marks, you might try to impress the instructor with your *bona fide* scholarship.

CHAPTER XXV

Inspiration

꿰꿰꿰꿰꿰

1. By taking care of your physical nature, you will be able to work with inspiration, with that drive which keeps you going until you finish the task. Yet you must be sure that you do not work yourself too hard, since every human being needs rest. Hence, you should learn to rest occasionally, but not excessively. A little self-analysis would help you to determine what form of recreation and relaxation would be best for you. You might find that attendance at sport events, either as spectator or participant, is your type of recreation. Or perhaps chess, crossword puzzles, music, or some other hobby may be more to your liking. Finally, plenty of sleep and good solid food are essential to keep your body in trim for the hard work of study.

2. It is a stimulating practice to have some mottoes for your own private help (but for no one else's eyes). Such could be: "Whatever is worth doing is worth doing well," or "Heroism consists in holding on for one more minute," or, "When all seems lost, attack!" There are many maxims like this, but most of them are sneered at by the

moderns as "copy-book maxims for school children." But, of course, the modern debunkers sneer at most of the good things that are older than yesterday. Their sneers should be taken as an accolade rather than a curse. Since mottoes are the summarized wisdom of the human race, they have spurred on many great men. It is only the man who hasn't the courage to keep trying who will laugh at the wisdom of those who have succeeded, and his laughter is always bitter and blighting—it is never constructive.

3.   Your aptitude or ability is not always measured by failures. For sometimes your failures are only an indication that you were untimely in your attempt, or wrong in your method, or too swift in your movement, or some other such reason. Someone has said that for every success, there have been ten previous failures. If you remember that, you will not feel too discouraged when things go awry. Let your failures be a challenge to further effort, not a cemetery where your ideals lie buried. You have only one life in which to accomplish a tremendous number of things. Therefore, you should not waste time regretting the past when you might be moving ahead; nor should you be so overwhelmed by the vision of the future that you give up all effort in the present. You never know to what heights you can rise until you try and keep trying.

4.   Have a favorite author or book to which you

can turn for inspiration when you feel the need. Inasmuch as none of us can keep going at top speed all the time, you will need an occasional boost for your energy and morale. No doubt you have noted certain books which have stimulated you when you first read them, and which continue to stimulate each time you turn to them. Keep such books handy—there will not be many. Open one of them occasionally at random and read for a while. The importance of this practice will be most notable when you have a difficult assignment ahead. The result will usually be renewed drive and stimulation for the mind.

5. Remember to pray. The student life is a temporary vocation in which you do the will of God if you apply yourself with all the ardor at your command. God will certainly help those who are sincerely bent upon perfecting themselves in their vocations. Praying as a real Catholic man, a follower of Christ, is as much a part of a student's life as is his application to his books. Pray to become great. There are too many mediocre men in the world, and not enough morally good men who are in all ways excellent. The need is for men who are inspired and inspiring. You should not be afraid to strive for such a goal.

CHAPTER XXVI

Attention

->>>->>>->>>-<<<-<<<-<<<-

1. You will more readily keep yourself in the habit of work if you convince yourself that your main occupation, and your constant preoccupation, must be your scholastic life. Anything not directly bearing upon your life of learning must be accepted as an intrusion—welcome or unwelcome, useful or useless, as the case may be. This habit of work is important to the process of focusing your attention during your study periods because it never permits your mind to wander very far from the main issue. Thus your mind does not have to make a long journey back when time for study arrives. The attitude just described may be expressed in the following words: "School is my life, and everything else—recreation, food, sleep, extra work —must be adjusted to fit into it." If this is your ordinary mental slant, periods of study will cease to be laborious stints from which you emerge with a grateful sigh. They will be accepted as your regular and normal routine.

2. In order to have an interest in the matter

studied, you must treat it as though it were important. If you approach each subject in your curriculum with respect, looking for the factors in it which make it significant, you will soon find the respect warranted by the impact of that subject upon history. No one forgets outstanding events in his own life. Since each subject of study is outstanding in some way, you will have to admit that it is worthy of your closest attention.

3. It will be good for attention's sake to respond actively to the subject matter. For example, try gesturing occasionally as you study, or declaiming the lesson to yourself. Imagine yourself to be in the picture, particularly if it be history, philosophy, or religion. Pretend that you are one of the persons present in a historical event, or that you are disputing with someone philosophically, or explaining a point of your religion to a non-believer. The matter will thus come alive and assist you to fasten your attention to it.

4. Practice excluding even perfectly harmless thoughts from your mind as an exercise in controlling your imagination. Much of a student's success in study depends upon the amount of self-control he has developed. If you have acquired a high degree of self-control, you will be able to make yourself pay attention when you feel least like it; and since all of you will experience days of being bored with study, you will be able to salvage some time that might otherwise be wasted.

5. Sometimes it helps toward concentration of mind to study with a sense of pressure. You should not do this regularly, but occasionally, in order to work yourself into the spirit of the subject. For example, give yourself one hour within which to master a particular chapter, or a group of problems. Make sure that the hour is barely sufficient. Forced thus to race against the clock, you will have little time to think of much else. This, as we have noted, is a remedial measure, not to be indulged in unless you have difficulty in applying yourself.

6. Close attention to the subject, which is sometimes called concentration, is greatly assisted by interest. Lack of interest breeds distractions. Yet there is, actually, no such thing as a distraction. What you commonly call distractions are, in fact, counterattractions. Being, at least for the moment, more attractive than your studies, they draw your mind to matters less profitable, if not dangerous. There is good sense, then, in making your studies as attractive as you can. Since each student is the best judge of what will attract him the most, you must analyze yourself to see whether you are drawn by the usefulness, delight in learning, competition with others, or the challenge of a difficult assignment. Whatever it may be, do not overlook its usefulness in keeping your mind to your work.

7. Similar to racing against the clock is the stratagem of occasionally setting a definite goal to be attained before you end a particular period of

study. For instance, you may propose to understand a certain battle in history, to explain to yourself a particular theory, to solve a problem in chemistry. When you have attained your goal, stop. You will gain free-time as a reward for diligence; you will have shorter periods of study; and you will maintain your interest at less cost in fatigue.

8. Limit your study periods to a two-hour maximum, followed by a short break. Since there is a point of diminishing return in the labor of study, you must not push yourself too hard over too great a stretch. It is better to take frequent breaks for rest (apparently losing time) than it would be to continue over lengthy periods with mounting ineffectiveness. This latter practice wastes time in the long run, and fatigues the mind. The existence of fatigue makes it impossible to be at one's best during recitations.

9. Competition in study is for some an incentive to interest and concentration. You may work with another student of nearly the same ability, and pit yourself against him. Be sure that you are of approximately the same ability or there will not be enough competition to keep interest alive. The effort to be more accurate, to work more swiftly, to show your superiority will bring out the best that is in you.

10. In order to learn as much as you possibly can, you should practice reciting your lessons, either to

yourself or to another. According to the old saying: "You do not know a subject until you have taught it," you stand your best chance of learning if you teach yourself by reciting to yourself or to a friend. Teaching a friend is preferable because you will be accountable to him, and your self-respect will spur you on. There is the added fact that since clarity is the sign of understanding, he can tell you whether or not you really know what you are talking about.

11. You will find that in spite of all your efforts, you sometimes fail to concentrate the way you would like. On such occasions, impose penalties upon yourself. These could take the form of going without a "coke," or a chocolate bar, or a cigarette, or something else you would enjoy. These penalties will have their full effect if you are certain that they will be exacted. These exactions will demand honesty, self-control, and the assurance that they will harvest a reward which will make the small sacrifices worth-while.

12. If you find that your mind continually wanders while you are studying, analyze yourself to discover why. It may be that you are worrying about some personal problem and, unknown to you, it is affecting your powers of concentration. Or, possibly, you are permitting distracting elements such as radios or nearby conversations to penetrate your study atmosphere. Again, you may not have sufficient interest in the subject that is

troubling you, or, for that matter, in any of your subjects. Self-analysis should give you the clue to the remedy.

13. Oftentimes during study periods, vagrant thoughts (but apparently useful ones!) come wandering into your mind. Proverbially these errant thoughts seem to be of great value. If you fear that you may lose them by present neglect, you can avoid the danger by keeping a supply of scrap paper handy. When the intruding thoughts come, jot them down for future investigation, and go on with your present work. This brief by-play will not be enough to cause a serious distraction, and yet you will have retained the essence of the distracting thought.

14. Another help to dissipate distractions is to take a short break, rise from your desk, walk about, wave your arms, and perform other physical actions calculated to loosen the grip of the distraction. After you have shaken it off, you can go back to your books in peace.

15. Do not study with anxiety. If you are worrying about your marks, or how you are ever going to finish the assignment, it will take most of your attention and energy needed for study. Proceed calmly, learn as much as you can, and use all the time at your disposal. Then leave the outcome to God. If you are doing an honest job, He will take care of the rest.

16. Since interruptions need not be distractions, do not be ready to thunder at some luckless person who interrupts your onrushing train of thought. You can, if you are really concentrating, handle minor interruptions without losing your mental balance. The real distraction is the one which grips you internally and captures your imagination. This is the one against which you must fight continually.

CHAPTER XXVII

Memory

·⫸⫸-⫸⫸-⫸⫸⫷⫷-⫷⫷-⫷⫷

1.   The memory works most efficiently when it is guided by the laws of association, which may be summed up under three headings: 1. the Law of Similarity, which means that those mental data which are in some way alike are more readily associated and, therefore, more easily recalled to mind; 2. the Law of Contrast, which states that those mental data which are in some way opposed are more readily associated and, therefore, more easily recalled to mind; and 3. the Law of Contiguity, which says that those mental data whose content has some proximity in time or space are more readily associated and, therefore, more easily recalled to mind. If, when studying, you will try to remain conscious of these three laws, your memory work will be greatly facilitated and your study will be less boresome.

2.   Since a way of life, with its power to form habits and shape thought patterns, has a profound effect on study, it will help your memory to pause each night before retiring and recall the incidents of the day. From this practice will grow a more

recollected spirit, one accustomed to reviewing portions of your life in orderly, precise fashion. The step from this evening period of recollection to recalling various elements of your studies is an easy one, as you will begin to remember in increasing detail the class periods of the day and, in rough outline, the contents of each period. As a result, it will not be long before you will grow into a man who is living a full, engrossing, and significant life.

3. The contemplative spirit, much needed in the world today, is fostered by the practice of recollection. Even the sketchiest acquaintance with the lives of great men will impress upon you the fact that they all were noted for reflective, interior (though not necessarily religious) lives. It is painfully clear that we live in an age of high speed which does not permit much depth of impression. Yet the needs of the life of the mind remain the same. You men who profess to be seeking a higher education must, therefore, go against the current. You must return within yourselves in order that your lives may be unified and coherent.

4. If the program we have proposed above becomes an integral part of your life, you will be well on the way toward bridging the gap between your formal studies and your daily life. It is the unconscious assumption of the student that his classroom subjects are, in a manner, removed from reality or actual daily living that makes them so

hard to remember. In reality, the customary short-sighted and harmful attitude of grudging admission of studies into an otherwise pleasant existence is the unreal approach. No wonder your lessons are hard to remember when they are treated as intruders! Just the opposite of this should be the rule. Your present life is one of study, and all things in your life should arrange themselves in subordination to your scholastic career. If you were to adhere faithfully to this proper hierarchy of values, your formal memory work would come more easily to you.

5. Since man is a rational animal, he will never be able to escape his rationality. He will instinctively stamp everything he does with the vestiges of his reason. Memorizing, being one of the activities of man, will also partake of this characteristic—the more so, the more properly it is done. Therefore, never try to memorize anything without first applying your understanding and reasoning powers to it. Be sure you know the meaning of every word used. Analyze the sentences and paragraphs for their structure and content. Make yourself familiar with the total picture first, before you start breaking it down into its component parts. If you thoroughly understand the material, most of the memory work has been done.

6. As we may say of practically every human endeavor, so also may we assert about memorizing—you will succeed at it in proportion to your will

to succeed. You must want to remember. There is no doubt that memorizing is usually distasteful because of the amount of drudgery connected with it. However, there are two solutions to this problem: 1. if you will approach memory work in the frame of mind and with the method here outlined, it need not contain so much drudgery; 2. if you will consider the rewards involved in the solid satisfaction of being able to recite a passage from memory as though it were a part of you, you may stimulate yourself to work harder. No matter what arguments you use on yourself, no matter what incentives you employ, you must make yourself want to memorize, want to remember, if you are to be at all successful at it.

7. If you approach memory work in a reasonable manner, you will realize that not everything needs to be formally committed to memory. A great deal of the initial survey mentioned in Number 5 above might consist of determining what to memorize and what to pass over. Many facts and ideas in a lesson are too trivial to burden the memory with. Many others of minor importance will easily return to mind because of their close association with the major items. There are always quite a few details which can be looked up when needed, or kept handy in a memorandum book for ready reference. Do not overburden your memory, and it will do a better job for you. The ability of a master is always attested by his knowledge of what to leave out.

8. First impressions are very powerful factors, both in forming prejudices and in stocking the memory. Hence, try to make your initial contact with what you are going to memorize both vivid and clear. While the vividness is important because the force of the impact causes the matter to remain embedded in the memory, the clarity of the impression has also its own great significance. Most things that are forgotten slip the mind because they were never clearly grasped. Material is clear when it is seen and understood in detail. The more details there are, the more hooks the matter has by which it may fasten itself to the memory.

9. Much of your incidental memory work, both during college and thereafter, will be the recollection of fragmentary material. This will comprise dates in history, definitions of terms, page numbers, names of books and authors, and other matters of the same class which fit naturally into no associative scheme. To remember these detached items, it will be helpful to fashion your own devices and classifications. For example, if yours is predominantly a sight memory, you might use colors or geometrical figures upon which to fasten the material to be remembered. If you have a better memory for sounds, you might try linking the subject matter with tunes or tones of voice, or something of the kind. The associations needed for the memorization of fragmentary and disconnected material will have to be constructed mechanically because of the lack of logical sequence.

Be sure to limit the amount of this sort of memory effort to that which is forced on you by necessity.

10.   It may happen that you will be asked to commit to memory passages of some hundreds of words. When facing this problem, you should be particularly careful of the method you employ. Never begin without having first surveyed the whole subject. Write an outline and make it rather detailed. Memorize the outline verbatim, for it is on this you will hang the remembrance of the rest. Once you have the outline memorized, go through it again and again, from beginning to end, adding the total content of the passage as you go. In this manner you will be redrafting the material for yourself, and it will be as though it were your own composition. Remember that the most important part of this technique is the thorough outline. If you draw that up and memorize it, the rest should not be too hard.

11.   The best method of committing a passage to memory has been found to be by taking it as a whole rather than in parts. The reason for this is that it does away with the awkward joints which are unavoidable if the material is memorized in sections which later must be linked together. Even when the passage is of considerable length, you should still follow this method, because you must endeavor to remember the passage as a unit. It should not deter you if you do not have time enough to complete the memorization at one sit-

ting. Come back to it at intervals, and work each time on the whole.

12. You will achieve better results if you limit your memory study to relatively short, but frequent periods. Because the mind tires in the effort to remember, brief spans of work will not cause so much fatigue. Intervals of rest will give the matter time to sink in, and the frequency of the efforts will have the good effect of reviewing.

13. When memorizing, put the matter in your own words first, before you attempt to assimilate the original. If you can express the subject in words of your own devising, you will make certain you understand it. Then, by the Law of Contrast, you should have an easier time remembering how the original author expressed his thought.

14. Frequent review is advisable if you wish to remember for any length of time. It has been found that review sessions are an excellent means of driving the material deeper into the mind. The efficacy of review rests on the same principle involved in your unconscious response to your own name, address, phone number. You probably never made any conscious effort to memorize the things most familiar to you. Yet, because they were constantly with you, their continued presence acted as a kind of perpetual review, until they became a part of your consciousness.

15. A safe way of proceeding is to overlearn. No matter how vivid the impressions made in the beginning, some of the material will fade with the lapse of time. To lessen the amount of loss, learn more about the subject, and memorize the subject more thoroughly than seems necessary to you at the time. If you stop just when you think you have it, you may find later that not all of it is there when you need it.

CHAPTER XXVIII

Making Notes

→≫→≫→≫‹‹‹-‹‹‹-‹‹‹

1. Every college student should train himself to make the proper kind of notes. Not a little of your scholastic success will depend upon the notes you have made from class lectures and recitations, from your extra readings, from private study, and from working out your own conclusions. For your perusal, therefore, we suggest the following fundamental considerations intended to assist you in making and keeping notes of all kinds.

2. The usefulness of notes comes from the fact that your memory cannot hold all that you are obliged to learn in your various courses. Much of the data you will learn is contained in books. However, not everything found in books is of importance to you, nor is it necessary to carry with you all the supplementary books you will use. Your notes will be a judicious selection made by you and kept for quick reference. Your viewpoint in note taking should be all-inclusive, that is, it should not be limited to the particular subject or subjects you are studying at present. Rather, your perspective should be broadened to ferret out all

useful material from your current reading. This material may include pertinent definitions, paragraphs of description, illustrative anecdotes, conflicting theories.

3. Another source of valuable notes is the class period. What occurs in class will, for the most part, not be found in writing anywhere. Yet, both the words of the instructor and the information gleaned from oral quizzes will commonly give you an abundance of matter worthy of being kept in note form. Therefore, a college student who would refuse to construct an orderly, complete, thorough set of notes from the material of his class periods would be throwing away the chance of a lifetime.

4. Since most professors will lecture in class in a conversational tone of voice and at a normal speed, you are going to be faced with a difficulty in taking notes under such conditions. Even if you were able to take shorthand (and that is not advisable), you would be hard pressed to keep up. The question is, therefore, what to do in order not to miss the important things which will be said? The preliminary answer to the difficulty is—do not try to take the lecture verbatim. First, the teacher himself does not expect you to do this. Many things he says are intended to be examples, or transitions, or obiter dicta by which he hopes to enliven the class, though they may not add anything to its learning. Such things as these need never appear in your note files. Again, the instructor will, as a rule, re-

peat important matter in different words and different ways. Do not repeatedly scribble the same thing under various disguises! If you endeavor to get down everything you hear, you will be so busy writing that you will fall far behind the lecturer.

5. It follows that you must have some way of selecting what you will preserve in note form, and what you will pass over. Reading ahead of the teacher in the textbook is one way of teaching yourself to be discriminating. Keep sufficiently far ahead of the place where the instructor is in class, and you will always know, as you listen to the lecture, what is new and what can be found in your text. Think how much feverish writing in class this will eliminate! Very often the instructor is merely rephrasing the thought of the text in order to make it more clear and more pertinent to his audience. Material of this kind should have no place in your notes unless it will give you new thoughts on the subject.

6. When reading ahead in the text, do not passively try to remember what the book says, but keep active by asking yourself questions about the thought development. Follow your author with curiosity, wondering what answers he will give to the questions which arise in your mind as you read along. Write the questions that occur to you on a piece of paper lest you lose them. They represent your original thinking, and holding fast to such products of your mind is important to you, even

though, in themselves, they may not be worth much. Any of these questions which are not answered by your textbook, or later, by the instructor in his lecture, should be proposed to the teacher. If they are aside from the class matter, propose them privately; if they are on the class matter, bring them up in class, for they may be of benefit to the whole group. The answers, whether you got them from teacher or book, should be recorded in your notes.

7.   Next, there arises the question of whether or not to rewrite the notes you have made in class. It might, perhaps, clarify the issue if instead of using the term *rewrite,* we were to speak of it as *revise.* Not every note you have will need revising; some of them will be clear and full enough as they are. Therefore, do not, for the sake of being methodical, waste any time changing them. However, there will be others which should be recopied, either because they are almost illegible, or because they are too sketchily made to withstand the erasing effects of time, or because they are incomplete and need to be filled out. Whatever the reason, do not hesitate to add to your notes, or to change them around, as the need or occasion arises. They should be, if they are to be useful, a dynamic collection of educational helps, and your way of manipulating them will make them exactly that.

8.   If you were a student devoted to your textbook alone, you would not have read as far as this;

hence, we shall add something by way of suggestion on the practice of supplementing notes. You will notice, as you move along, that theories change with the discovery of new facts, and that new facts are always coming to light. You will read newer and better books which will clarify and expand your present knowledge. Other teachers will have clearer and more forceful ways of explaining the matter you have already covered. Do not hesitate to add all these bits of knowledge to your notes, even though you have already completed the course to which they belong. Learning is not compartmentalized, although teaching methods may be. Education never ceases, and your notes should reflect the development of your mind.

9. Speaking of active participation in your own education by the development of notes leads naturally into a discussion of research. Perhaps you have seen a connection between two subjects in your curriculum and would like to investigate; or perhaps there is some point in the material you are now studying, or have studied in the past, which intrigues you, and into which you would like to delve more deeply; here are your research projects! Here is an extra-curricular activity second to none! There is not only a feeling of satisfaction in working your way to profound intellectual depths, but there is also the experience of organizing original material, and the practice in self-control necessary to force yourself to stick to it, even though there seem to be insuperable difficulties. You will proba-

bly never be in a better position or in a more congenial atmosphere for undertaking research (unless you become a professional research worker) than while you are at college. A well-stocked library is ready at hand for your use, and an abundance of expert counselors is within easy calling distance. Every student should engage in some research while in college, because, in addition to reaping the benefits already mentioned, he will also grow in appreciation of men who have succeeded at what he has tried and found difficult.

10. As you set out on your voyage in research, first look at the project as a whole. Organize it from beginning to end. Analyze it thoroughly and divide it into parts so that you may have manageable portions to handle. You should make a list of all the available literature on the subject, and establish and learn the techniques necessary to complete it. As you work, be patient with yourself, and do not expect too much right at the start. Since all good things take time, do not be surprised if it takes you a little while to establish proficiency. No matter what, do not give up! Carrying through to a finish that which you have begun will add to your educational stature in every way.

11. Facts and items of information will differ in value. There are main facts, coordinate and subordinate facts, theories, opinions, deductions, conclusions, and hosts of other instruments of research. If you are scrupulously exact in distinguishing one

from the other, you will be much more likely to employ them according to their value, and not as though they were of equal value. When making up your notes, set off these different items in a manner that will mark their worth. At all times separate examples and illustrations from facts and arguments, lest, mistaking pictures for thought, you try to prove your point by merely giving an example of it.

12. There is more to any subject than the main theme or idea. Within all intellectual pursuits there is a depth which is practically unfathomable, wherein the searcher after truth finds himself in the midst of a bewildering wealth of ideas, led on step after step, from thought to thought, until there seems to be no end to his findings. It will not do to permit yourself to be beguiled so far from the main thought that your project ends in chaos. Nor, on the other hand, should you despise altogether the side lanes and byways of research which beckon you on, for this would be not only to deprive yourself of much pleasure, but also of much important learning. Many scholars have come upon their most important discoveries while investigating one of these side issues.

13. Any note you think worth keeping should be preserved in proper style. Do not merely write something down and store it away, for that will surely lead to much jettisoning of unintelligible script at some future date. Each note you keep

should be properly identified. Write on it the source of the note—book title, author's full name, publisher and year of publication, name of magazine and article, page note was found on—as well as the date of taking the note, because the latter will sometimes have an important bearing on its meaning. Following upon the note itself, it would be well to indicate your reason for making this particular note, as well as your impression of it at the time you made it. This will give you a kind of self-evaluation which, if continued in all your notes, will describe the progress of your thought up to the present moment.

14. Your notes should be kept in outline form, unless some special consideration dictates otherwise. The completeness of the outline will depend upon the importance of the subject-matter, and upon how much of it is habitual memory with you. Yet, although it is in outline, it should not consist of a series of disconnected jottings without any grammatical coherence. The sentences should be complete, as a rule; exceptions may be permitted in places where you are certain clarity will not suffer thereby.

15. There will be times when you must decide whether to copy out complete quotations, or to make paraphrases of the material. No all-embracing rule can be given. In general, a paraphrase in your own words is better, not only because it will be shorter, but also because (since notes are to be

understood as well as preserved) forcing yourself to make the paraphrase will contribute to your full understanding of the content. On the other hand, you will certainly come across passages which will lose much of their force and charm if put in any other way than the author's These you should take verbatim; be sure to copy them exactly, down to the last comma and period. Later, when you may have occasion to use this material, never fail to make exact reference to the source—whether you are quoting it verbatim or in a paraphrased version—since justice and your own integrity demand this of you. Once you have gathered a fair sized anthology of quotations from your favorite authors and subjects, you can gain quite a bit of inspiration and consolation from reading it periodically.

EPILOGUE

. . . Atque Vale!

THERE is little more to add. The purpose of this book has been, as we have said, to give you something to keep which you may pore over repeatedly. From it you will be able to learn your profession of studenthood thoroughly. It would be foolish to attempt a college career without the intention of putting your best into it. Your life in college can, and should, be happy. There is no reason for it to be a period of grind, worry, doubt, or frustration. Yet, even though you may be having a wonderful time while you are a student, do not, therefore, miss the underlying seriousness of the life.

As you read these pages, you may conclude that we have set before you an impossible ideal. Even while admitting the truth of our observations, you may have been unable to rid yourself of the feeling that we were expecting too much of human nature —youthful student nature, that is. Such hesitancy on your part is understandable. For the accepted standards of the day condition you to expect the minimum attainment from everybody, rather than the maximum from the few. To put it another way: instead of concentrating on lofty ideals which will entice the strong into soaring with them, the men of our times advertise a respectable least-common-denominator for success, in order to encourage the weak to keep trying. Both aims are laudable, but neither should be stressed at the expense of the other.

Let us remind you of a further consideration, namely, that a Catholic should not permit himself to give in to a life of comfortable anonymity. Since you profess to have God as your Father, you ought to face up to the responsibilities of the family tradition. Provided you put forth your best efforts, there is no limit to what you may expect of yourself. Set your ambitions high—higher, even, than you have any expectancy of reaching, because you may always depend upon the help of God when you are serving Him. Only He knows what is out of your reach, and, because He wants you to keep trying, He will not tell you until you have come before Him for your reward. Try your wings thoroughly before resigning yourself to walking to heaven.

When you follow your ideals, you will almost certainly be tempted to discouragement at meeting with failure. Yet, everyone must fail part of the time. This is a condition of life. But failure makes the man—on the proviso that he continues to labor in spite of failure. Were you to get by in college with no scars to show for the effort, you would have missed much of the educational benefit to be gotten from overcoming odds. Life in this world will never be easy, and the college, if it is to do its work properly, must teach you to conquer in the rough game of life.

Index

A

Absence from class, 25-26
Activities
  extra-curricular, 18, 37-42, 151, 152
  religious, 33-36
  social, 39-42, 151
Accuracy
  in making notes, 201-203
  in reading, 83, 155, 157-158, 159
Aesthetics, area of education, 121-129
Alcohol, use of
  See Drinking
Analysis
  of self, 18, 79, 150, 177
  process of, 110-112, 127-128
Assistantships, 66
Association, process in memorization, 187, 191
Athletics, 4, 43-46
Attention, 87, 149, 169-171, 180-186
Attitude
  toward college, 3-8
  toward memorization, 189-190
  toward reading, 158-160
  toward teachers, 27-30

B

Beautiful, the
  See Aesthetics
Bibliographies, 168
Boarding in college, 60-63
Books
  evaluation of, 156-157, 167-168
  kinds of, 53-54
  of reference, 167
  textbooks, 58, 144
  withdrawal of, 57, 164-165

C

Campus
  boarding on, 60-63
  care of, 50-51
Careers, 64-69
Catalogue, library, 164-165
Christian education of youth (Pius XI) 31
Christian Doctrine, Confraternity of, 35
Class
  absence from, 25-26
  attention in, 87, 170
  attitude during, 19
  note taking in, 196-197, 198
  promptness for, 25
  recitation in, 102

Collateral material, 142-143
College
  attitude toward, 3-8
  newspaper, 37
  objectives of, 11-12, 14, 18
  proms, 39-40, 41-42
  reputation of, 51
Compositions
  See Writing
Comprehension
  in reading, 85-86, 156-159
  of lecture, 87
Concentration of mind, 149, 182
Confraternity of Christian Doctrine, 35
Contemplation, 188
Control
  of emotions, 172-173
  of environment, 134-135
  of others, 131, 133-135
  of self, 44, 103-104, 145, 181
Conviction, intellectual, 113-114
Copyright law, 166-167
Courses in religion, 31-32, 117
Courtesy, 40-41, 95
Cramming, 21-24
Creative reading, 155-156
Creative work, 124-129
Curriculum, 16, 24-25
Cut system, 25-26

D

Dances
  See Social Activities
Deafness, psychological 86-87
Development
  in self control, 44, 103-104, 131-132, 145, 181
  intellectual, 11-13, 73-75, 174
  of sense of hearing, 86-88
  of synthetic power, 124-129
  of total man, 74-76
  physical, 11-12
  spiritual, 32-36
  See also Contemplation, Mortification, Prayer, Self-Analysis
Dewey decimal system, 161-163
Difficulty of study, 21-22
Discipline, 44, 103-104, 130-137, 145, 181
Distractions, 146-147, 182, 184-185
Dormitories
  See Boarding in College
Drinking, 41

E

Education
  aesthetic, 78, 121-129
  Catholic objectives of, 31-36
  different from training, 14-15
  disciplinary, 78, 130-137
  formal, 13-14
  informal, 13-14, 28, 65
  liberal, 76
  of expression, 78, 94-104
  of impression, 78, 80-93
  of thought, 78, 105-114
  philosophy of, 74
  purpose of, 11-12
  religious, 23-28, 78, 115-120
Effort, 126-127, 145, 207-208
Emotions, 172-173
Emphasis in writing, 99
Encyclical, Christian education of youth, 31
English, 143

See also Expression, Grammar, Literature, Vocabulary, Writing
Enunciation, 102-103
Environment for study, 146-174
Essay on criticism, 4
Examples, use of in study, 175
Expenses of student, 41-42
Expression
area of education, 78, 94-104
in study, 149-150
oral, 101-103
tone of voice, 102
written, 96-101
Extra-curricular activities, 18, 37-42, 151, 152

F

Failure, lessons from, 178, 208
Feelings, education of, 88-90
Fellowships, 66
Formal education, 13-14
Fraternity house system, 61-62

G

Gang spirit, 18-19
Gesture, 103
Goals
See Objectives
Good taste, 121
Government, student
See Student Council
Graduate schools
See School
Grammar, 84-85

H

Habits of study, 23
Hearing, development of, 86-88

History, 126, 143
Holy Name Society, The, 35

I

Ideals, 173-174, 207-208
Ideas, origin of, 80, 106-107
Imagination
in reading, 54, 155-158
in study, 181
Impression, area of education, 78, 80-93
Inattention, 184-185
Indecision, 89-90, 141-142
Index, use of, 158
Informal education, 13-14, 28, 65
Information, classification of, 175, 200-202
Integration, 24-25
Intellectual development, 11-13, 73-75, 174
Interest
in learning, 169-170, 180-181
in writing, 99-100
Intramural sports, 44
See also Athletics
Introspection
See Self-Analysis
Intuition, 113-114

J

Judgment, training of, 155-156, 172-173

L

Law
observance of Divine, 118-119
of Copyrights, 166-167
Laymen, educated, 3
Leadership, 36

Learning, interest in, 169-170, 180-181
    See also Study, Training
Lecture
    comprehension of matter, 87-88
    method of teaching in college, 19
Liberal education, 76
Librarians, 54-55
Library
    at home, 58
    catalogue, 164-165
    periodicals in, 165-166
    reading room in, 56-57
    reference books in, 167
    withdrawal of books from, 57, 165
Library of congress system, 163-164
Literature, 126
    See also English, Expression, Grammar, Vocabulary, Writing

M

Magazines, 165-166
Memorization
    association in, 187, 191
    attitudes towards, 189-190
    in study, 188, 191, 192-194
    recollection in, 187-188
    techniques of, 108-110, 187-194
Memory, faculty of, 108-110
Methods
    in research, 166-167, 199-200, 201
    of memorization, 108-110, 187-194

of study, 21-26, 145-154, 159, 175-176, 177-178, 180, 181, 183, 193-194
Mortification, 88-89, 145, 147
Mottoes, use of, 177-178

N

Neatness, 123, 147
Newspapers
    college, 37
    in library, 166
    in study, 142-143
Notes, 19, 144, 195-203
    format of, 201-203
    from books, 197-198, 199
    from class, 195-197, 198
    revision of, 198

O

Objectives
    in study, 141-144, 182-183
    of Catholic education, 31-36
    of college, 11-12, 14, 18
    of education, 11-12
    of primary and secondary schools, 11-12
    of student, 15, 24
Observation, 91-92, 169-171
Outlines in study, 148-149
Overemphasis of athletics, 45

P

Paragraphs
    See Writing
Penance
    See Mortification
Persistence, 126-127, 145-146
Pius XI, 31
Philosophy of education, 74
Physical development, 11-12

Planning
  for life, 126
  in study, 175-176
Prayer, 179
Primary schools
  See School
Professional schools
  See School
Promptness
  for class, 25
  in study, 147-148
Proms
  See Social Activities
Pronunciation, 102-103
Property, care of, 50
Purposes
  See Objectives

Q

Qualities of student, 23-24
Quotations, anthology of, 203
Questions in class, 152

R

Reading, 83-86, 155-160, 197-
    198
  accuracy in, 83, 155, 157-
    158, 159
  attitude toward, 160
  breadth in, 156-157
  caution in, 160
  comprehension in, 85-86, 156-
    159
  creative, 155-156
  depth in, 157, 159
  for inspiration and relaxa-
    tion, 178-179
  judgments formed by, 156
  of periodicals, 165-166
  oral interpretation in, 84

speed in, 83-84, 155
Reasoning, 106-108
Recitation
  during study, 183-184
  in class, 102
Reference books, 167
Reflection, 112-114, 188
Relationship
  of subjects, 24-25
  student-teacher, 27-30, 48, 153
Religion
  area of education, 31-36, 78,
    115-120
  study of, 31-32, 119-120, 154
  Tradition, Sacred, 116
Religious activities, 33-36
Religious vocation, 67-69
Reputation
  of school, 16, 51
  of teachers, 27-30
Research, methods in 166-167,
    199-200, 201
Responsibility
  for property, 50-51
  in study, 74-75
  personal, 18-19
Revelation, divine, 116
Review in study, 23, 149, 150-
    151, 193
Roommates, 62

S

Schedule for study, 148
Scholarships, 66
School
  graduate, 15, 66
  primary, 11-12
  professional, 15, 66
  reputation of, 16, 51
  secondary, 11-12, 17

School spirit, 47-49
Self-analysis, 18, 79, 150, 177
Self-control, 44, 103-104, 131-132, 145, 181
Self-denial, 88-90, 145, 147
Sentences
  See Writing
Social activities, 39-42, 151
Sodality, 34-35
Specialization, 15, 66
Speech, faculty of, 95, 101-103
Spirit of the gang, 18-19
Spiritual development, 32-36
Sports
  See Athletics
Student
  activities, 33-42, 151, 152
  expenses of, 41-42
  objectives of, 15, 24
  qualities of, 23-24
Student council, 49-50
Student-teacher relationship, 27-30, 48, 153
Study, 73-79, 146-147, 153-154, 175
  and extra-curricular activities, 38
  competition in, 183
  concentration in, 149-150, 182
  cooperation in, 133-134
  cramming, 21-24
  difficulty of, 21-22
  environment for, 146-147
  habits of, 23
  interest in, 180-181
  main object in life, 180, 188-189
  mastery of subject, 152-153

methods of, 21-26, 145-154, 159, 175-176, 177-178, 180, 181, 183, 193-194
objectives of, 141-144, 182-183
planning in, 175-176
rest from, 177, 183, 185, 193
review, 23
schedule for, 148
warm-up for, 150-151
See also Education, Lecture, Notes
Subjects
  mastery of, 152-153
  relationship of, 24-25
Syntax, knowledge of, 84-85
Synthesis, process of, 124-129

T
Teacher-student relationship, 27-30, 48, 153
Teamwork, spirit of, 44
Technique
  classroom, 19
  of memorization, 108-110, 187-194
  of research, 166-167, 199-200, 201
Textbooks, 58, 144
Thought, area of education, 78, 105-114
Tradition, Sacred, 116
Training
  different from education, 14-15
  for careers, 64-69
  of judgment, 156, 172-173
Transition from secondary school, 17-20
Typewriting, 26

V

Verse
  See Writing
Visual aids, 159
Vocabulary, 84, 96-97, 155
Vocation, religious, 67-69
Voice expression, 101-103

W

Words
  See Vocabulary
Work, creative, 124-129

Writing
  attractiveness in, 100-101
  clearness in, 98-99
  force in, 99
  interest in, 99-100
  of compositions, 97-98
  of paragraphs, 97
  of sentences, 97
  of verse, 98
  See also English, Expression,
    Grammar, Literature, Vo-
    cabulary

A NOTE ON THE TYPE
IN WHICH THIS BOOK IS SET

This book is set in Baskerville, a Linotype face, created from the original types used by John Baskerville, the eighteenth-century typefounder and printer. This type has long been considered one of the finest book types ever developed. The letters are wide and open and have a businesslike approach. The finer hairlines give exquisite delicacy. The heavier strokes give color and strength. The relation of the two in combination gives a brilliant effect and makes for easy reading. The book was composed and printed by the Wickersham Printing Company of Lancaster, Pa., and bound by Moore and Company of Baltimore. The typography and design are by Howard N. King.